SCHOLASTIC

Teaching About
Nonfiction
With Picture Books

BY CONSTANCE J. LEUENBERGER

NEW YORK • TORONTO • LONDON • AUCKLAND • SYDNEY
MEXICO CITY • NEW DELHI • HONG KONG • BUENOS AIRES

Teaching
Resources

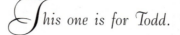

This one is for Todd.

ACKNOWLEDGMENTS

*I would like to give special thanks to my editor, Joan Novelli,
and to Deborah Schecter for making this book what it is.*

Book cover from MARTIN'S BIG WORDS: THE LIFE OF DR. MARTIN LUTHER KING, JR.
by Doreen Rappaport, illustrated by Bryan Collier. Text copyright © 2001 by Doreen Rappaport.
Illustrations copyright © 2001 by Bryan Collier. Reprinted by permission of Hyperion Books for Children.
All rights reserved.

Book cover from WAITING FOR WINGS by Lois Ehlert. Copyright © 2001 by Lois Ehlert. Reprinted by
permission of Harcourt, Inc.

Book cover from WAKE UP, WORLD! A DAY IN THE LIFE OF CHILDREN AROUND THE WORLD
published by Frances Lincoln Ltd. in association with Oxfam, copyright © 1999. Published in the U.S. by
Henry Holt and Co.

Editor: Joan Novelli
Cover and interior design by Kathy Massaro
Interior art by James Graham Hale

ISBN-13: 978-0-439-66119-5
ISBN-10: 0-439-66119-6

1 2 3 4 5 6 7 8 9 10   40   15 14 13 12 11 10 09 08

Contents

Teaching Nonfiction Using Science-Related Picture Books

Teaching Nonfiction Using Social Studies-Related Picture Books

About This Book

$\mathcal{M}$OST OF THE READING PEOPLE DO IN THEIR LIFETIME IS NONFICTION. Keeping this in mind, it makes sense to teach children the features and functions of nonfiction text. Nonfiction text requires abstract thinking, questioning, drawing inferences, extrapolating ideas, and synthesizing information, just to name a few skills! In this book you will find a wealth of activities and ideas to support children in navigating successfully through nonfiction text. Whether they're learning how a penguin protects an egg in *The Emperor's Egg*, mapping migration paths in *Waiting for Wings*, or investigating the Montgomery bus boycott in *Martin's Big Words*, children will be actively building a strong base for reading and writing nonfiction.

Using notable nonfiction books as a teaching tool, the activities in this book are designed to provide support for helping children build background knowledge, develop strategies for previewing text, acquire new vocabulary, and learn how to make sense of nonfiction text. In addition to exploring text structure (such as comparisons and time order), children will learn about text features, including headlines, boldfaced and italicized words, diagrams, maps, charts, timelines, sidebars, tables of contents, glossaries, and indexes.

What's Inside?

In the following pages you'll find lessons to extend students' understanding of the features and functions of nonfiction books in both the science and social studies realm. Here's a look at the features you'll find for each title.

◎ **Story Summaries:** An introduction to the book highlights prominent features of nonfiction.

◎ **Before Reading Activities:** The ideas here guide students in previewing text and constructing a reading road map. Discussion starters and activities build background knowledge and scaffold students' learning.

◎ **During Reading Activities:** Questions about the text help students monitor their comprehension during reading.

◎ **After Reading Activities:** Ideas for discussion help readers review, sort, and synthesize information. Step-by-step activities provide for further learning about features of nonfiction and strengthen students' skills across the curriculum.

◎ **Vocabulary Focus:** Vocabulary instruction helps deepen children's understanding and encourages a curiosity about words that will further their word knowledge.

◎ **Book Links:** Encourage continued exploration of the topic with the teacher-tested titles in this annotated list.

Using Nonfiction With Early Learners

Children have a natural thirst for information. Many children choose to read nonfiction text, longing for their questions on a certain topic to be answered. When students come to print with their own questions and reasons for reading, they are truly engaged with print. Once children start reading nonfiction text, they learn more about their world, which leads to better understandings, more connections, deeper knowledge, and, in the end, a higher level of learning. Why include nonfiction as an integral part of any primary reading program? There are many compelling reasons.

❋ We live in an information-based society. Adults tend to read more nonfiction than fiction. If we are to prepare our children for this world, it only makes sense to teach children the features and functions of nonfiction.

❋ As children progress through the grades, they will encounter more and more nonfiction texts as a primary source for learning new material. When teaching younger children nonfiction reading strategies, we are preparing them for their educational journey, and the demands of life ahead.

❋ Children who read nonfiction have an increased knowledge of the world.

❋ Nonfiction text naturally lends itself to the teaching of vocabulary, extending students' language abilities.

Creating a Classroom That Supports Nonfiction Inquiry

There is a strong connection between classroom setup and the learning that occurs within it. When teachers fill their classrooms with rich learning opportunities and authentic items from the real world, they create an excitement for and love of learning that is contagious. Information-rich classrooms include:

❋ Centers that invite exploration of items from nature, such as stones, shells, leaves, fresh flowers, and vegetables

❋ Pets and plants for companionship and scientific observation

❋ Information resources such as calendars, dictionaries, encyclopedias, magazines, catalogs, phone books, maps, globes and atlases, travel brochures and fliers about museums and attractions, and charts, graphs, and tables

❋ Tools such as notebooks, clipboards, highlighters, sticky notes, binoculars, microscopes, magnifying glasses, tape recorders, overhead projectors, and video and digital cameras

Teaching Tip

The Internet offers access to Web sites that can enrich and enliven learning on almost any topic. Before having students access any of the Web sites referenced throughout this book, please preview them first as content and Web addresses may change over time.

Teaching Tip

Classroom current-events magazines are rich sources of material for reinforcing features of nonfiction. For more practice, after a lesson on any nonfiction feature, send children on a treasure hunt to find books or articles with the same feature. In advance, make sure to have materials with the target feature on hand.

Bibliography

Beck, I. L., McKeown, M. G., & Kucan, L. (2002). *Bringing words to life: Robust vocabulary instruction*. New York: Guilford Press.

Duke, N. K. & Bennett-Armistead, V. S. (2003). *Reading and writing informational text in the primary grades: Research-based practices*. New York: Scholastic.

Farnham, D., Jensvold, P., & Kulhowvick, B. (2007). *Mini-lessons for teaching about nonfiction*. New York: Scholastic.

Wilhelm, J. D. (2001). *Improving comprehension with think-aloud strategies: Modeling what good readers do*. New York: Scholastic.

Choosing Nonfiction Texts for Early Learners

The children's nonfiction book market has exploded in recent years, and the choices available for teaching nonfiction in the primary classroom are extensive. But how do you choose the best nonfiction texts for your students? Here are a few guidelines.

✳ Make sure the text will hold students' interest.

✳ Decide what your goal is for teaching nonfiction features. If it is to teach headings and special fonts, be sure the text you choose offers plenty of these features.

✳ Check the accuracy of the text; information can change quickly. To help with this, check the copyright date of the book.

✳ Use books that are at the reading level of your students; make sure they can understand the language. For read-alouds, choose books at a level slightly above students' reading levels.

Connections to the Language Arts Standards

The story pages in this book are designed to support you in meeting the following standards as outlined by Mid-continent Research for Education and Learning (McREL), an organization that collects and synthesizes national and state curriculum standards, and proposes what teachers should provide for their students to grow proficient in language arts, among other curriculum areas.

Reading

- Understands how print is organized and read
- Uses mental images based on pictures and print to aid in comprehension of text
- Uses meaning clues to aid comprehension and make predictions about content
- Uses phonetic and structural analysis to decode unknown words
- Understands level-appropriate sight words and vocabulary
- Knows main ideas or theme, setting, main characters, main events, sequence, and problems in stories
- Summarizes information found in texts (retells in own words)
- Makes simple inferences regarding the order of events and possible outcomes
- Relates stories to personal experiences

Writing

- Uses drawings to express thoughts, feelings, and ideas
- Writes for different purposes
- Gathers and uses information for research purposes
- Generates questions about topics of personal interest
- Uses a variety of sources to gather information

Source: *Content Knowledge: A Compendium of Standards and Benchmarks for K–12 Education* (4th ed.). Mid-Continent Research for Education and Learning, 2004.

In addition, the activity pages in this book support components of the Reading First program (U.S. Department of Education): phonemic awareness, phonics, vocabulary development, reading fluency, and reading comprehension strategies.

Biggest, Strongest, Fastest

by Steve Jenkins

✿✿

(TICKNOR AND FIELDS, 1995)

From a tiny flea to the mammoth blue whale, the animals in this book set records for being the biggest or the smallest, the fastest or the slowest, and everything in between. Each page compares the animal to a human in a small diagram, helping children to compare and contrast the unique characteristics of the animals to themselves.

Before Reading

Preview the Text

While flipping through the pages of the book, point out the format the author uses to compare an animal's characteristics to human characteristics. Explain that comparing something we know to something we don't know can help us understand a topic better. The illustrator uses two types of art in this book, cut-paper collage art, which depicts the physical characteristics of the animal, and a diagram, which depicts its size, strength, or speed in relationship to a human. Ask these questions to guide students in taking a closer look at the way these illustrations work:

✳ In which picture is the size of the animal easier to visualize? Why?

✳ Which picture makes it easier to visualize the physical characteristics of each animal? Why?

✳ How do both types of illustrations help readers learn about the animal?

Building Background Knowledge

Ask students if they know of an animal that is remarkable in some way. For example, children may have seen an ant carrying a large crumb, much bigger than the ant itself. They may have learned fascinating animal facts from reading a book or watching television. Invite students to share any facts they know about animals, accepting all answers. Explain that animals do amazing things and that this book will share many interesting animal facts.

Teaching Tip

When children have the opportunity to observe animals for extended periods of time, they quickly learn amazing facts about the way certain animals live. If you are able, arrange for students to observe animals in the classroom for a day, a week, or even the year! Invite families to share their pets—"borrow" a hamster, guinea pig, or another animal for the day. Ant farms are also relatively easy additions to a classroom menagerie. Encourage students to observe the animals and take notes.

Because the main text of this book is very user-friendly for early readers, it lends itself well to teaching some beginning reading strategies. Before prompting students to follow a text with their finger, this reading strategy must be taught: While reading the selection aloud to students, point to each word as it is read, explaining that this helps readers keep their place as they read each word. If multiple copies of the book are available, invite children to follow along as you model the strategy. Reinforce awareness of the text structure by inviting students to visualize the comparisons the author makes for each animal.

After Reading

Children will be eager to discuss their opinions about amazing animals. Use their enthusiasm to reinforce concepts in the book, and to focus attention on comparisons.

1. Invite students to share with a partner the page they liked best. Encourage them to identify any comparisons the author made and to use details to support their views.

2. Bring students together for a whole-class discussion. Allowing students to first share with a partner gives them a chance to try out and clarify their ideas before sharing with the group. Beginning with a partner share also gives all students a chance to be heard, even if they do not have an opportunity to contribute to the class discussion.

Finding the Essentials (Science, Language Arts)

Charts are an important graphic in nonfiction text, informing readers of vital information. Take a closer look at charts to help children learn more about how to use them.

1. Revisit the chart at the back of the book. Explain that this chart provides a quick guide to the essential information in the book. (If needed, partially copy the chart on a whiteboard for easier visibility.)

2. Ask questions about animals that children can answer by reading the chart—for example, "Which animal is the tallest?" "Which animal is found in Cuba?" "Which animal eats mammals' blood?" As children answer the questions, have them point out where they located the information on the chart.

Record Breakers (Science, Language Arts)

Many of the animals in this book are Olympians in their own right. Use the book as inspiration for students' own nonfiction books about record-breaking animals.

1. Review the record-breaking categories in the book (biggest, strongest, fastest, and so on).

2. Guide students in researching animals that break records—for example, the largest insect, the smallest fish, the fastest bird, and the loudest land animal. Give each child a copy of Record Breakers (page 11). Have children complete the sentence to name their animal and tell what record it breaks. Then have them fill in three facts (size, diet, range) and draw a picture that compares their animal to something.

3. Have students share their completed pages and then work together to compile them into a class book, complete with a front and back cover and a contents page, as well as any other features they are familiar with (such as a glossary or an index).

Teaching Tip

Which is the loudest animal in the sea? On land? Meet these and other animal record-holders, including mammals, birds, fish, reptiles, and invertebrates online at the National Zoo (nationalzoo.si.edu).

Animal Chart (Science, Language Arts)

Encourage students to try their hand at creating a nonfiction graphic. After students have researched animals that break records, and the class book is complete (see Record Breakers activity, above), make a chart similar to the one at the back of *Biggest, Strongest, Fastest*.

1. Set up a chart with the following categories: animal, record, size, diet, range, other.

2. Have children take turns adding information for the animals they studied.

3. Add a copy of the completed chart to the back of the class book.

Animal	Record	Size	Diet	Range
Blue Whale	loudest animal	82–105 feet 200 tons	krill	the world's oceans
Arctic Tern	longest migration	11–15 inches 3–4 ounces	small fish	Arctic North America and Eurasia to Antarctica

How Big? How Small? (Math)

Students will enjoy this activity that revisits the author's use of comparisons (as a text structure), and enhances science and math skills.

1. Refer to the pages of *Biggest, Strongest, Fastest* as reference, and calculate the sizes of the featured animals.

2. Use measuring tools to measure out the size of an Etruscan shrew, a bee hummingbird, a bird spider, and so on. (For the larger animals,

(continues)

Teaching Tip

To take this activity further, use large art paper to create animal cutouts to scale, with the blue whale being largest and the flea being smallest. Display in order by size.

Keep in Mind...

▲▲▲▲▲▲

A "wonder list" is an effective strategy for teaching children to self-monitor their comprehension. As they read, have them respond to the text by saying "I wonder why...." They might be able to answer their questions as they continue reading, or they might find they need to revisit some text to get a better understanding. Wondering "why" may also inspire children to undertake further investigation on their own.

Book Links

•••••••• ◆ ••••••••

Amazing Animal Facts
by Jacqui Bailey, Joe Elliot, and Jayne Miller (Dorling Kindersley, 2003): This information-rich classroom resource features photos of each animal.

Exploding Ants: Amazing Facts About How Animals Adapt by Joanne Settel (Atheneum, 1999): Vivid photographs make this a great read-aloud!

What Do You Do With a Tail Like This? by Steve Jenkins and Robin Page (Houghton Mifflin, 2003): This Caldecott Honor book offers interesting tidbits about animals, including how a lizard's tail breaks off in self-defense and why some fish have four eyes.

such as a blue whale, take the measuring outside and use chalk or string to mark off how large the animal is.)

3. Encourage conversations that involve comparisons. How does the author help readers visualize the size of a bee hummingbird? What comparisons can children make to better grasp the size of the smallest of all birds?

Wondering About . . . (Language Arts, Science)

How do anacondas swallow whole deer and goats? This book will raise a lot of intriguing questions for young readers about what else animals can do, making this a good time to introduce a "wonder list."

1. At the top of a sheet of chart paper write the words "We Wonder...." Invite students to call out things the book made them wonder about. Record responses. Note that students might also wonder about what other animals can do. Record these ideas as well.

2. Use the questions on the chart as springboards for discussions, and as topics for further research.

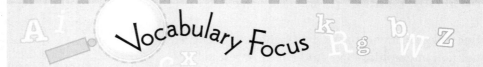

Build students' vocabulary for words that describe how some animals defend themselves, or prey on others.

> **poisonous:** To be capable of producing a substance that can cause death or illness.

> **shock:** A muscular spasm caused by an electric current passing through the body.

1. Revisit pages of the book that use these words (the sun jellyfish, the bird spider, and the electric eel). Invite students to share what they think the words mean. Encourage them to study illustrations and reread text to understand the meaning.

2. Guide students to a definition of the words as used in the book. Discuss other meanings and uses of the words as well.

3. Add the words to an illustrated science vocabulary word wall. Play word wall games to reinforce students' ability to use the words. Say, "I'm thinking of a word that..." and fill in some characteristic of a word, such as a definition ("I'm thinking of a word that means...") or a word-part feature ("I'm thinking of a word that contains the smaller word *poison*").

Name _____ Date _____

Record Breakers

The _____ is the _____ .
(animal)   (record)

Size: _____
_____
_____

Diet: _____
_____
_____

Range: _____
_____
_____

Teaching About Nonfiction With Picture Books © 2008 by Constance J. Leuenberger, Scholastic Teaching Resources

The Emperor's Egg

by Martin Jenkins

(CANDLEWICK PRESS, 1999)

Can you imagine balancing an egg on your feet for two months in subzero temperatures without any food? The male emperor penguin does just that! This book explains the chick-rearing habits of the emperor penguin and is chock-full of facts about these amazing animals. It also includes an index to help students sharpen their alphabetizing and research skills.

Before Reading

Preview the Text

Look at the pages with children, pointing out the pictures. What does the emperor penguins' environment look like? What information do the illustrations give readers about Antarctica? Invite students to share their reactions to the pictures. Offer prompts, such as "How do you think you would feel living in Antarctica where these penguins live?" Call attention to the italics at the bottom of some pages. These italics are extra facts the author has added about emperor penguins. Show the index at the back of the book and explain that it is used to quickly find information in a book.

Building Background Knowledge

Invite children to share what they know about penguins and Antarctica. Together, locate Antarctica on the globe. Share the following facts to build students' background knowledge before reading.

* Antarctica is an island (land surrounded by water on all sides).
* The North and South Poles are both very cold, but we often think of going "south" to get warmer.
* The South Pole can reach 70 degrees below zero with winds up to nearly 200 miles per hour, which is much colder than the weather in North America.
* Penguins only live in the Southern Hemisphere.
* Penguins are birds, although they don't fly; they use their flippers to swim.

Teaching Tip

▲ ▲ ▲ ▲ ▲ ▲

Children understand complex ideas and concepts better when they have been given time to freely explore and play with related materials. In support of this, fill a sensory table or several plastic tubs with water and ice cubes. If large chunks of ice or snow are available from outside, they make wonderful additions to this exploration station. Add thermometers, salt, measuring receptacles, and items that sink and float. Let children explore and experiment with the materials.

As you read, pause after every two or three pages and encourage discussion about the text. Invite students to share their thoughts about the amazing life of emperor penguins as you probe the basis of their thought processes with question such as "Why do you think so?" How do you know?" and "Where does it say that?" Point out the words in italics on the pages as you read, explaining that when a font changes, it signals to the reader "Pay attention! This is important."

After Reading

Emperor penguins have a challenging and interesting life. Ask the following questions to elicit children's reactions to what they have learned.

✳ Did you find it unusual that the father took care of the egg and the newborn chick? Why?

✳ Do you think the mother and father penguin shared the job of raising their young fairly? Why do you think so?

✳ How was the information in the italic text different from the standard text? How did this help you understand more about emperor penguins?

How Blubber Works (Science)

Emperor penguins are very well adapted to withstand freezing temperatures. Their special feathers provide a very warm, waterproof "coat," and they have a layer of blubber that also protects them from cold. Try this experiment to help students understand how blubber works to keep penguins warm.

1. Fill a container with ice water. Place a scoop of vegetable shortening in another container.

2. Invite students to thoroughly cover an index finger with the shortening, then place two fingers in the cold water, one finger with the shortening coating and one bare. What do they notice? Discuss observations and share hypotheses about how blubber works to keep penguins warm. (Blubber acts as an insulator to help penguins maintain their body temperature.)

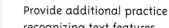

Provide additional practice recognizing text features such as italicized or boldfaced type. Have children pair up and look through books for font changes that signal important vocabulary or information. They can mark pages with sticky notes and share them with the class.

To help students generate facts about the emperor penguin, integrate a mini-lesson on using an index. Model how to use the index to locate different topics. Begin by identifying a topic and looking page by page for information. Then use the index to locate the page number and the information. Have students explain which method works better. Continue, having students suggest topics of interest and letting them take turns using the index to locate information. Add the facts to the class list.

Name _____ Date _____

Penguin Fact Sheet

[blank box]

This is an emperor penguin.
Emperor penguins live in _____.
They are about _____ tall.
They eat _____.
Three more facts about emperor penguins:
1. _____.
2. _____.
3. _____.

Only the Facts (Language Arts, Science)

To help children understand the difference between fiction and nonfiction text, try this writing activity.

1. Discuss with students the difference between fact and fiction. Guide them to recognize that *The Emperor's Egg* is based on fact.

2. Using *The Emperor's Egg* as reference, create a class-generated list of facts about emperor penguins.

3. Using the class-generated list and a think-aloud approach, write an informational paragraph about emperor penguins. For example, as you write, think aloud about the organization of facts you choose to include.

4. Invite students to use the facts to write their own informational paragraphs about emperor penguins. Younger children may also draw a "true" picture of emperor penguins and write one fact about them. Teachers will need to assist with this, accepting phonemic spellings and scribing as needed.

Penguin Experts (Language Arts, Science)

Along with *The Emperor's Egg*, provide nonfiction books on the topic for further investigation (and for practice with nonfiction features).

1. Set up a display of books about emperor penguins (see Book Links, page 15). Invite students to use sticky notes to mark interesting pages. They can initial the sticky notes to make it easy to return to those pages.

2. Work with small groups to guide students in researching facts about emperor penguins. Have students complete a Penguin Fact Sheet (see sample, left) to report on their research (using words and pictures). Remind students that it is important to draw "like a scientist," using details to make the penguin drawings as realistic as possible. Students can label their drawing to show important parts of a penguin.

It's a Bird! It Has Feathers! It's a Penguin! (Science)

A penguin is an odd animal that often confuses many adults, not to mention children. Is it a mammal? A fish? A bird? Some children will have a hard time distinguishing what category penguins fit into, mistaking their tightly grouped feathers for fur or skin, and equating their swimming abilities with being like fish. A comparison of the three types of animals will help clarify matters.

1. Give each child a copy of the facts cards (page 16).

2. Discuss each group of animals, encouraging children to make comparisons among them—for example, they may notice that birds and fish lay eggs, but mammals do not. Discuss what it means to be warm-blooded (blood remains at a constant temperature, regardless of environment), and that only mammals nourish young with milk.

3. Invite students to add one more piece of information to each card, something that will help them remember the differences between birds, fish, and mammals.

A Penguin's Problem (Science, Movement)

To help children understand the difficulty in carrying an egg around on feet all day, let them try it out!

1. Let children take turns balancing a ball on their feet as they waddle like a penguin around the room.

2. Discuss how balancing the ball is like a penguin balancing an egg. Invite children to share what it was like to keep the ball balanced on their feet. Then have them imagine what would be different if they had to balance it in the cold on slippery ice.

Vocabulary Focus

Strengthen descriptive vocabulary by taking a closer look at words in *The Emperor's Egg* that tell how penguins move. Revisit pages of the book that use the following words.

huddle: To crowd together, including for warmth.

shuffle: To walk while dragging one's feet.

trundle: To move slowly and heavily, in an uneven way.

Invite students to share what they think these words mean. Encourage them to look at the illustrations and reread text for meaning clues. Review the meaning of each word. Then invite children to join you in acting out the words as you move like penguins. Add the words to a word wall (for words that describe movement). Invite children to copy them into a vocabulary notebook.

Keep in Mind...

▲ ▲ ▲ ▲ ▲ ▲

When selecting vocabulary words to teach, choose those that will be useful to students not only while reading the current selection, but while reading other selections, and in their own writing as well.

Book Links

• • • • • • • • • • • • • •

The Emperor Lays an Egg by Brenda Z. Guiberson (Henry Holt, 2001): This beautifully illustrated book follows a family of penguins through a typical year.

Penguins! by Gail Gibbons (Holiday House, 1999): Find fascinating facts about penguins, including their habitats, lifestyles, and nesting habits.

Penguins (Face-to-Face series) by Stuart Lafford (Scholastic, 2002): The clever use of transparent pages lets readers come face to face with penguins as they build nests, take care of their young, and keep warm.

It's a Bird! It Has Feathers! It's a Penguin!

Mammal

- Walks, flies, or swims (usually walks)
- Has hair or fur
- Warm-blooded
- Babies are born live
- Nourishes young with milk
- Uses lungs to breathe
- _____

Fish

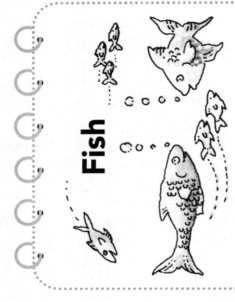

- Swims
- Has scales
- Cold-blooded
- Lays eggs
- Uses gills to breathe
- _____

Bird

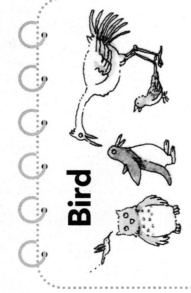

- Usually flies, sometimes swims, or does combination
- Has feathers
- Warm-blooded
- Beak, no teeth
- Lays eggs
- Uses lungs to breathe; one-way breathing system
- _____

The Shortest Day
Celebrating the Winter Solstice

by Wendy Pfeffer

❧

(DUTTON, 2003)

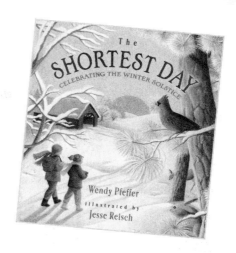

Each year, during the winter months, the sun rises later and sets earlier, culminating in the winter solstice, or the shortest day of the year. This book explains the winter solstice in scientific terms, and introduces how other cultures have understood the changing seasons. Diagrams help readers visualize important information.

Before Reading

Preview the Text

Take a "picture walk" through *The Shortest Day*, and invite students to share their ideas about what the book might be about. Point out the placement of the sun in the pictures and ask children what they think the sun has to do with the book. At the back of the book, share the diagram of Earth rotating around the sun. Ask students what this picture has to do with the pages in the rest of the book. Continue with questions such as:

❋ In what season do we see the sun more?

❋ In what season does it get darker earlier?

❋ What do you think this book has to do with the sun?

Building Background Knowledge

In preparation for sharing the book, guide students in thinking about the relationship between the sun and the seasons.

1. Invite students to make connections between the seasons and their own activities. Ask:

   ❋ What is your favorite season? Why?

   ❋ What activities do you like to do in summer?

   ❋ What is your favorite winter fun?

   ❋ Why do you think you might do some activities more often during certain seasons? (For example, if they like to play outside

(continues)

Keep in Mind...

Before- and after-reading activities for *The Shortest Day* are modeled on the "Experience -Text- Relationship" instructional approach (Tharp, 1982; as cited in Duke & Bennett- Armistead, 2003). First, students gain *experience* with concepts in the book through the globe and lamp demonstration (page 18). After reading and discussing the *text*, students make *relationships*, or connections, between the demonstration and the text. For more instructional strategies with nonfiction texts, read *Reading and Writing Informational Text in the Primary Grades: Research-Based Practices* by Nell K. Duke and V. Susan Bennett-Armistead (Scholastic, 2003).

and ride their bike in summer, but didn't choose this activity for winter fun, their reasoning might be that it gets darker earlier in winter and there isn't as much time to play outside.)

2. Explain to students that the activities they do in each season often have a lot to do with how the sun shines on Earth. Illustrate this with a simple demonstration.

1 Have children sit in a circle. Place a globe in the center. Shine a flashlight on the "globe." Explain that the light represents the sun.

2 Tilt the North Pole away from the "sun." Explain to students that it is now winter in North America because the North Pole is tilted away from the sun. In South America it is summer, and much sunnier.

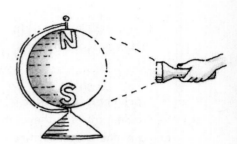

3 Holding the globe tilted in this way, have a helper move it around the sun. At another quarter turn, point out that the sun is shining equally on both poles, so it is spring.

4 Continue with the tilt another quarter way around the sun, and explain it is now summer in the Northern Hemisphere. The sun is shining more on the north, with the Southern Hemisphere receiving less light.

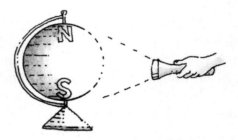

5 Another quarter turn around the sun and it is fall as the sun shines equally on both poles.

During Reading

To activate background knowledge while reading, remind students of the globe and flashlight demonstration (above). You might first read the book without interruptions, and then reread it to make connections, pausing to explain the demonstration as it relates to the text. As you read, use the globe to locate places the author references. Guide students in noticing how the diagrams provide information that supports the text.

After Reading

Use these discussion starters to encourage students to make connections between the demonstration (page 18) and concepts in the book.

✳ The early people were afraid because it was getting darker and darker during the winter. What would you tell them about what was happening with Earth and the sun?

✳ Why do you think the sun seems to set at different places on the horizon at different times of the year? What does that have to do with our globe and flashlight demonstration?

Pictures Are Important (Art, Language Arts)

Explore with children how pictures in nonfiction books support the text. Revisit pages in *The Shortest Day* and focus attention on the illustrations. What information do they give children about the subject matter? Deepen their awareness of the way pictures and text work together with an activity that lets them further explore this feature of nonfiction.

1. Revisit the illustration with the calendar showing the date "December 21." Invite children to describe what they see, and then use inferencing skills to fill in additional details about what's happening. For example, there is a cup of hot cocoa on the table, which might indicate it is cold outside. Children may also conclude that there is someone in the house, though this person is not shown, and that the boy looking in the window may be on his way in to warm up.

2. Have children write (or dictate) and illustrate a sentence about the shortest day of the year. Encourage them to explain how their illustrations (example at right) give information that their sentences do not.

Seasonal Flowchart (Science, Language Arts)

Flowcharts are organizational tools that frequently appear in nonfiction text. To help students better understand how to use this graphic tool, revisit the flowchart in *The Shortest Day*. Then have children complete one of their own. Note that the concepts contained in the flowchart included in *The Shortest Day* may be too abstract for young children to grasp. The reproducible flowchart offers a simpler version that allows children to focus on developmentally-appropriate concepts as they gain experience with this feature of nonfiction.

1. Give each child a copy of the Seasonal Flowchart (page 21). Guide children to notice the organization of the chart and the use of arrows to show the order of the seasons.

(continues)

Teaching Tip

In the winter, the days get shorter and the nights get longer. When children can't play outside, time seems to drag. Help children combat these winter blues by brainstorming activities they can do to keep their bodies and minds active—for example, they can write letters, play board games, and read more books! (This is also a great way to create some alternatives to watching television!)

My puppy and I warm up by the fire.

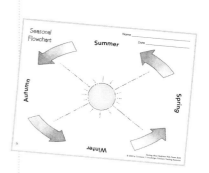

2. Have children complete the flowchart by drawing a picture in each section of something they like to do in that season.

3. Let children practice reading their completed flowcharts with a partner, making connections between the seasons and activities they enjoy at different times of the year.

Solar Power (Language Arts, Science)

Thousands of years ago ancient people would name the powers of the sun to explain how the sun helped them. Invite students to do the same, while they also learn about a different type of graphic organizer: the web.

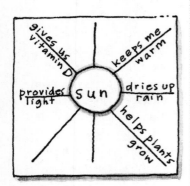

1. Introduce the concept by creating a chart-size "sun" web (see sample, left). Think aloud as you complete each portion of the web: Write the word *sun* at the center. Along each ray, write ways the sun helps people.

2. Using the class sample as a model, have each child make a "sun" web on a sheet of paper. Have children complete the web by using words (and pictures, if desired) to tell how the sun helps them.

3. If students like, they can share stories about how the sun helps them, using each ray as a prompt to tell a different part of their story.

Book Links

The Return of the Light: Twelve Tales From Around the World for the Winter Solstice by Carolyn McVickar Edwards (Marlowe & Co., 2000): Explore the winter solstice with mythical tales from many cultures.

The Winter Solstice by Ellen Jackson (Millbrook Press, 1994): Learn about ancient customs and beliefs surrounding the winter solstice and connections to present-day celebrations. For a look at the longest day, share Jackson's *The Summer Solstice* (Millbrook Press, 1994).

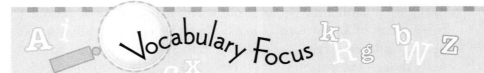
Vocabulary Focus

Young children can aurally understand much more sophisticated words than they can read. For this reason, before, during, and after reading *The Shortest Day*, it is important to explain words that children may not know. Revisit the following words in the text. Have students tell what they know about the words. Provide additional explanation as needed.

astronomer: A scientist who studies space.

horizon: The place where the earth and sky meet (or as scientists say, where they "apparently" meet, as they don't actually meet).

solstice: From the Latin word *sol*, meaning sun, and *sistere*, meaning to stop; where the sun reaches its highest or lowest point.

tilt: To tip slightly.

Deepen students' knowledge by providing oral practice with the new words. For example, use a word in a sentence, and include an error (such as a mispronunciation). Have students listen for and correct the error.

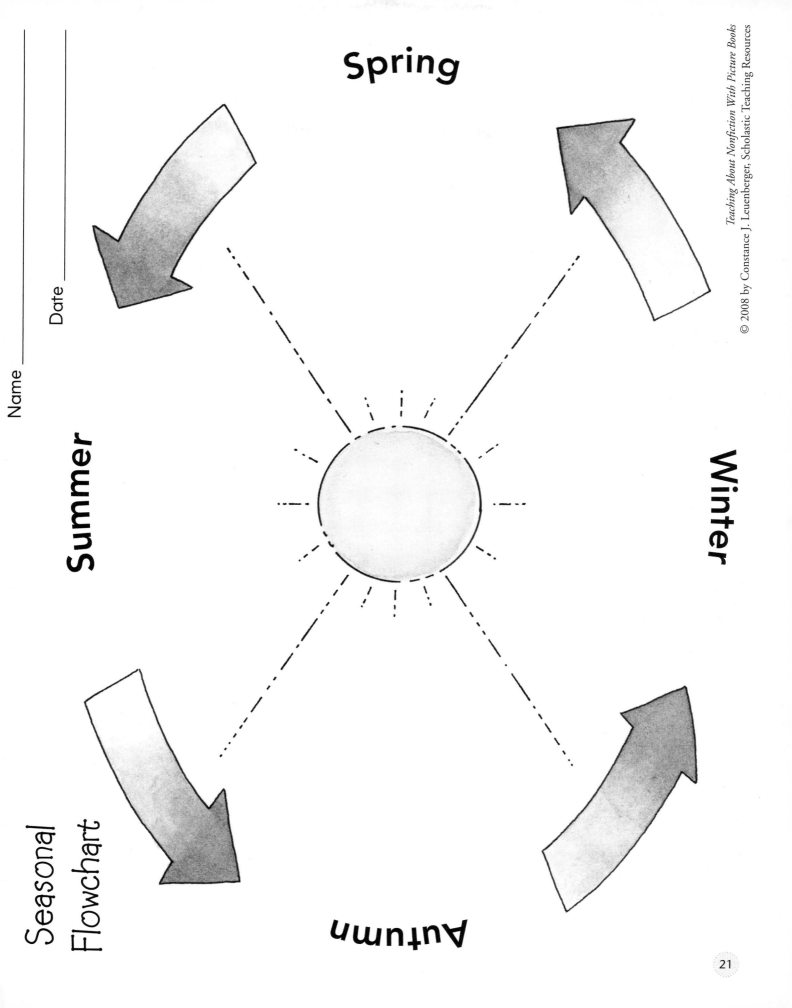

Name _____

Date _____

Seasonal
Flowchart

Spring

Summer

Winter

Autumn

Teaching About Nonfiction With Picture Books
© 2008 by Constance J. Leuenberger, Scholastic Teaching Resources

Tell Me, Tree
All About Trees for Kids

by Gail Gibbons

❧❧

(LITTLE, BROWN, 2002)

This book is packed with information about trees and includes many diagrams and labels, important features of nonfiction text. Readers learn about the functions of different tree parts, types of fruits and seeds, uses for trees, and more. Highlighted terms are also identified in illustrations.

Before Reading

Preview the Text

Before reading, direct students' attention to the many diagrams in the text. In each case, invite students to identify what they think the author is trying to explain. Tell students that a diagram is a picture that an author uses to show parts of something, or to explain how something works. Sometimes arrows or lines are used to draw attention to specific parts of the picture. Explain that authors use diagrams to convey a lot of information in a small amount of space, and that diagrams help readers visualize ideas to make them easier to understand and remember.

Building Background Knowledge

Create some tree lovers with this informative activity!

1. If you are able, before reading the book, take a brief walk around your school's neighborhood or playground to look at trees in the area. This can spur a discussion about different types of trees. If you are unable to take a walk around and look at trees, view pictures in guidebooks (see Book Links, page 23) and talk about different types of trees that children have seen.

2. Create a K-W-L chart. First, ask children what they already know about trees and record their information on the chart (under "K"). Next, ask children what they want to learn about trees and record that under the "W" column on the chart. The "L" portion of the chart (indicating what they've learned) will be filled in after reading (see After Reading, page 23).

During Reading

Because this book is loaded with diagrams, it's a good idea to stop as you read and carefully explore these graphic aids. Point out labels, explaining to students that when they see a label in bold or italicized text, it is a sign to the reader that something important is being discussed. Note that these boldfaced or italicized words also often appear in a glossary. This book contains more information than can be absorbed in one reading, so plan on reading it aloud several times, revisiting it as needed during your study of trees.

After Reading

Although the K-W-L chart will not be complete until your study of trees is complete, it's a good idea to add some information after reading the book.

1. Discuss with children what they learned from the book and add that to the "L" portion of the chart.

2. The book may have also brought up more questions for children. Record these under the "W" portion of the chart. Discuss ways students can find answers to their questions, including doing research using other sources.

3. Finally, compare and contrast the book to narrative text. Ask: What looks different about this book? What things do you see in this book that you don't usually see in storybooks? Why do you think the author chose to write this book this way? What are some things the author included that were helpful to you, the reader?

My Tree (Science, Language Arts)

Invite students to take a closer look at trees and the way diagrams help readers visualize information.

1. Go outside and have each student choose a tree to study. (More than one student can study the same tree.) If you are unable to go outside for this activity, provide guidebooks (see Book Links, above right) and other resources and let students choose a tree to "observe."

2. Give each child a copy of the tree diagram template (page 26). Revisit diagrams in *Tell Me, Tree*, and review with students how their diagram is like the diagrams in the book.

3. Have students cut out the labels at the bottom, glue labels for trunk, bark, branch, limb, root, and root hairs in the boxes, and then draw arrows to the corresponding tree parts. Students can use the extra labels, including the blank, to further diagram their tree. Have children complete the diagram by adding details that are specific to their tree, such as leaves or fruit.

Book Links

Are Trees Alive? by Debbie S. Miller (Walker, 2002): Take a trip around the world to learn about trees in different countries. At the end, readers will find a map for locating places discussed in the book.

Peterson First Guides: Trees by George A. Petrides (Houghton Mifflin, 1998): Two hundred and forty-three common trees of North America are represented in this field guide. Plenty of pictures and diagrams make this a great resource for the classroom teacher!

Red Leaf, Yellow Leaf by Lois Ehlert (Harcourt Brace, 1991): This book follows a sugar maple tree through its life. An appendix provides information regarding the care and biology of trees.

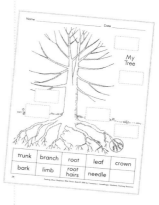

Measuring Trees (Science, Math)

Have students try their hands at measuring trees.

1. Give each child a small ball of string, a tape measure or yardstick, and a pair of blunt scissors.

2. Take students outside to measure their tree (see My Tree activity, page 23). Have them wrap the string around the base of the tree to measure the circumference (cutting the string to show the circumference), and then repeat at a point about two feet above the base. Students can pair up to help each other with this process. Provide students with masking tape to label their strings (with their name and from which point the measurement was taken—at or above the base).

3. Have children bring their strings inside and tape them to a sheet of paper. Children can then measure their strings with standard measuring tools (such as yardsticks or tape measures) and record the circumference at each point.

4. Gather students together and invite them to graph their measurements. To do this, have them tape their strings to a chart from smallest to largest. Graph measurements from the base and those from higher up separately. What conclusion about how trees grow can children draw based on the information they gathered?

5. To transfer this information to their tree diagrams (see My Tree diagram, page 26), use arrows and labels to record the circumference at each point.

Trees Make Food (Science)

Revisit pages in *Tell Me, Tree* that explain photosynthesis. Chlorophyll stored in plants is what enables them to make their own food. Using microscopes to look through a thin section of a leaf, invite students to look for little green "jelly beans." These are cells called chloroplasts that are filled with chlorophyll. Next, to actually see chlorophyll, try this demonstration.

1. Place a fresh, green leaf on top of a wood board approximately 5 by 5 inches.

2. Next, place a piece of white cotton fabric on top of the leaf (old bed linens cut up work great!). Tack the cloth to each corner of the wood.

3. Gently pound a hammer on the cloth, following the outline of the leaf. As cell structures are broken inside the leaf, chlorophyll will seep through the fabric, creating an outline of the leaf.

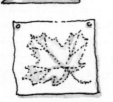

4. To preserve the outline on the fabric, lightly mist with vinegar and press with a hot iron (adult use only). Display in the classroom as a lovely reminder of the way trees make food.

Leaf Peepers (Science, Math)

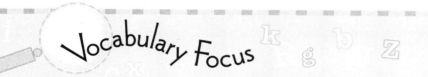

Try this graphing activity to help children identify different types of leaves, and to provide practice presenting and reading information in a format that is common to nonfiction reading material.

1. Take students outside to gather different types of leaves from the school grounds. (If this isn't possible, collect leaves and bring them to school for students to examine.)

2. Explain to students that scientists classify leaves as wavy, lobed, toothed, or smooth. Provide several samples of each type (mixed up) and let children group the leaves according to the type they think they are. Share characteristics of each type and let children revise their groupings as necessary.

3. Create a graph on a large sheet of paper. Establish the leaf categories by placing one of each type of leaf at the bottom of each graph line. Label each category.

4. Invite children to place the leaves on the graph according to type. Ask questions to help children interpret the data, make comparisons, and draw conclusions: "How many wavy leaves are there?" "How many more toothed than smooth?" "What does this graph tell us about the trees in our area?"

Vocabulary Focus

Tell Me, Tree offers many opportunities for building science vocabulary. Revisit pages in the book that use the following words.

chlorophyll: The matter in the leaves that makes the leaves green, and that gathers the sunlight to make the food.

conifer: Trees that keep their seeds inside cones and have needles are called conifers. These trees usually stay green throughout the winter. A Douglas fir is an example of a conifer tree.

deciduous: Trees that lose their leaves in the fall are deciduous. They typically have broad leaves. Oak, maple, beech, and birch trees are examples of deciduous trees.

photosynthesis: The process by which leaves of a tree use sunlight to make food for the tree.

Invite children to read the words with you several times. Let children look for clues in the text and illustrations that help them understand the meaning of each word. For example, students may connect the words *conifer* and *cones*, and use what they know to make sense of the new word.

Keep in Mind...

"We consider the best sources for new vocabulary to be trade books that teachers read aloud to children rather than the books children read on their own. . . in contrast to introducing words before a story, in our work with young children we have found it most appropriate to engage in vocabulary activities after a story has been read" (Beck, McKeown, & Kucan, 2002).

Name _____ Date _____

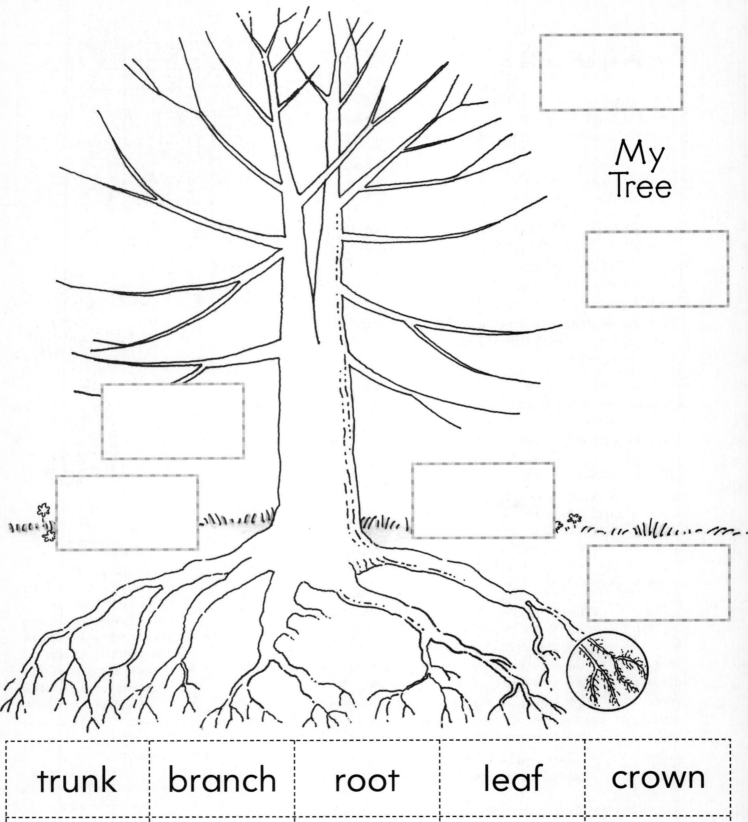

My Tree

trunk	branch	root	leaf	crown
bark	limb	root hairs	needle	

Waiting for Wings

by Lois Ehlert

(HARCOURT, 2001)

"Out in the fields, eggs are hidden from view, clinging to leaves with butterfly glue." So begins this bold, breathtaking picture book that chronicles the story of caterpillars' metamorphoses into butterflies. A mini-book within the book tells the story of the caterpillars, with the pages becoming larger as the butterflies emerge. The endpages provide information on butterfly identification, general facts about butterflies, diagrams, and other useful data.

Before Reading

Preview the Text

Read the title of the book and ask students to predict what the book is about. Next, flip through the pages of the book as students follow along. Note the different sizes of the pages and ask students why they think the author chose to make the pages different sizes. (*The pages represent the newly morphed butterflies.*) Share the diagrams at the back of the book and ask children why they think these are included. (*Diagrams help the author explain important information in a small amount of space.*)

Building Background Knowledge

Scaffold students' learning by asking them to share with a partner times they have seen butterflies or caterpillars, or something they know about the subject. Having students share their ideas with a partner creates an atmosphere where everyone has a turn to talk. It also gives students an opportunity to develop an appreciation for the knowledge they each have. As students discuss, listen carefully to their conversations to determine the extent of their experiences and background knowledge about butterflies and caterpillars. When the discussion is over, fill in gaps as needed so students can understand the text.

During Reading

This text lends itself well to using a think-aloud strategy, because it is quite simple and easily reread for clarification.

Teaching Tip

How big can butterflies be? How small? Guide students in measuring and marking a 5/8-inch line on a sheet of paper, the size of one of the smallest butterflies, the eastern pygmy-blue. Have students measure and mark 12 inches, the size of one of the largest butterflies, the birdwing butterfly.

(*continues*)

Keep in Mind...

▲▲▲▲▲▲▲

Think-alouds are reading strategies in which a reader models what good readers do by explicitly teaching the thought processes, including what the reader is thinking, feeling, wondering about, and noticing during reading. Let the phrase "Hmm" signal that you are switching from reading to think-aloud mode. Begin think-aloud statements with "I predict," "I think," "I wonder," or "I'm confused" as you guide students through the text. A good source of additional information is *Improving Comprehension With Think-Aloud Strategies: Modeling What Good Readers Do*, by Jeffrey D. Wilhelm (Scholastic, 2001).

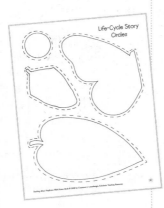

Life-Cycle Story Circles

1. The first time through the reading, demonstrate a think-aloud by drawing attention to interesting phrases, such as *butterfly glue*. State your wonderings aloud—for example, "Hmm, butterfly glue, I wonder if that is something that really exists. What is it?"

2. Continue reading and pause when you read, "Each one knows what it must do." Say, "Hmm, I think I might know what they must do—find a place to make a cocoon. Let's see if I'm right about that."

3. Continue, questioning the text, and at times answering yourself, demonstrating what good readers do when they are engaged with the text. Make sure that students know that it is okay to ask questions while reading, and to not always get the answers; the process of the think-aloud helps to make better readers.

After Reading

Book Talk

After completing a think-aloud version of the read-aloud, reread the book and invite students to share their questions regarding the text. Have students compare their own questions and comments with the ones you raised in the think-aloud.

❋ How are the questions similar? Different?
❋ What questions would they still like answered?

Life-Cycle Story Circles (Science, Art, Language Arts)

Create paper-plate story circles students can use to retell the story of a butterfly's life cycle. Give each child a copy of the patterns (page 31) and a paper plate, and then guide children in following these steps.

1. Cut out the patterns to represent the four stages of the butterfly life cycle: egg, caterpillar, chrysalis, butterfly.

2. Glue a cotton ball to the leaf pattern. This represents a butterfly egg.

3. Trace and cut out four or five circles using black, yellow, and green construction paper. Arrange the circles to form a caterpillar and glue them together where they overlap. Glue on wiggly eyes. Staple pipe cleaners in place to make antennae.

4. Cut a chrysalis from green construction paper. Use gold glitter glue to make a thin line along the top of the chrysalis and three dots near the bottom, to represent a monarch chrysalis's shiny appearance.

5. Fold a sheet of orange construction paper in half and place the wing pattern on the fold as indicated. Cut out the wing and open to reveal a full butterfly. Dot paint on one butterfly wing, then fold in half to make the mirror image on each side. Add wiggly eyes and pipe cleaner antennae to complete the butterfly.

6. When dry, attach the back of each piece to the outer area of the paper plate, in life-cycle order. Let students pair up and take turns using their story circles to tell a butterfly life-cycle story.

Teaching Tip

Encourage students to use their story circles as reference to write about the life cycle of a butterfly. Tape or glue the story to the center of the plate.

Butterfly or Moth? (Science, Language Arts)

Many children have trouble distinguishing between a moth and a butterfly. Use a Venn diagram to help them understand the differences.

1. Plan a trip to the library to help children locate sources of nonfiction information that tell about moths and butterflies.

2. Draw a large Venn diagram on chart paper. Have children share facts about moths and butterflies. Together, decide if the information applies only to one or the other or both. Add it to the appropriate area of the Venn diagram (see sample, right).

3. Invite children to use the Venn diagram to construct comparisons—for example, "Moths rest with their wings spread. Butterflies rest with their wings together."

4. Make a connection to diagrams as a feature of nonfiction, explaining that authors use diagrams like this to help readers make sense of information. Let children work with partners to locate diagrams in books and share them with the class.

Teaching Tip

▲▲▲▲▲▲

To further reinforce content area vocabulary and use of glossaries, have students work with partners to prepare an entry for a glossary to go with *Waiting for Wings*. Have students work together to arrange their words and definitions in alphabetical order.

Map the Migration (Science, Social Studies)

Using and reading maps are an important skill in understanding nonfiction text. Put these skills to work by mapping the migration of the monarch butterfly (or another type of butterfly, if you prefer).

1. Millions of monarchs make the trek to Florida and Mexico each year to escape the chilling temperatures of the northern regions. Guide children in using nonfiction resources to follow their migration path on a map. A good source of information is Monarch Watch (www.monarchwatch.org).

2. Post a map of North America on a bulletin board. Provide children with lengths of yarn and thumbtacks. Let them map migration routes as they learn more about them.

3. Revisit the map often to let children "read" the map. Where do monarchs migrate from? To? What places do they pass through?

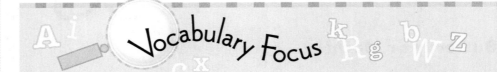

Stretch students' vocabularies by highlighting content area vocabulary in *Waiting for Wings*. Revisit pages of the book that introduce the following words.

chrysalis: The protective shell that the caterpillar forms around itself, sometimes called a cocoon.

larva: The beginning stage of an insect—a caterpillar, in the case of a butterfly.

metamorphosis: A life change, such as from a caterpillar to a butterfly.

Invite children to say the words with you and to share what they know. Provide additional information to enhance their knowledge. Add the words to a butterfly word wall (write words on paper cut into butterfly shapes), and play games to reinforce word recognition. For example, say, "I'm thinking of another word for *cocoon*." (*chrysalis*)

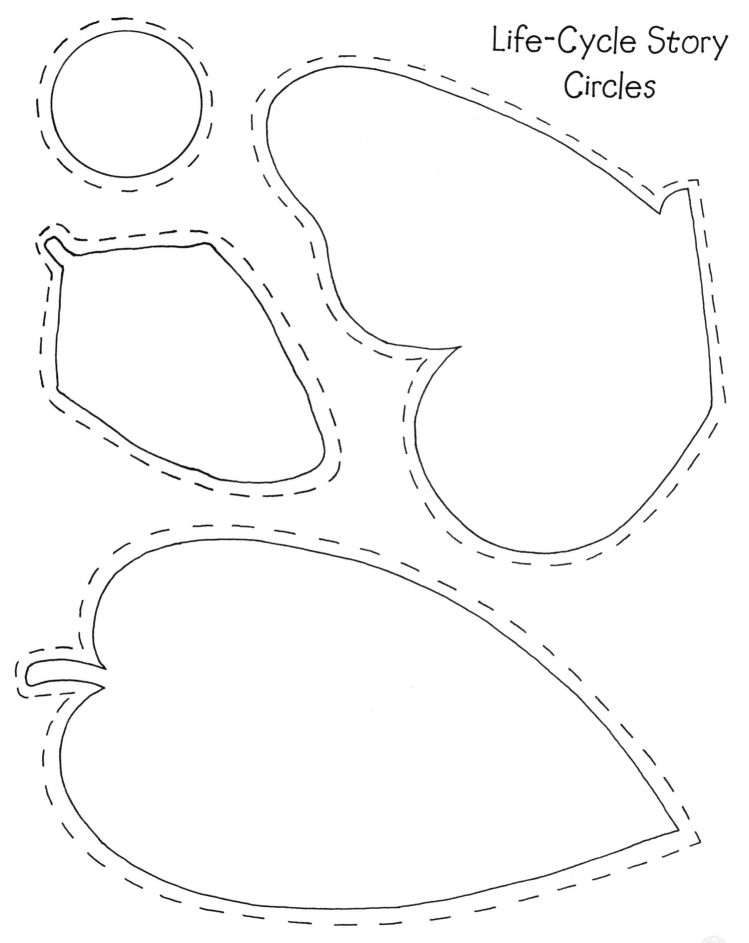

Life-Cycle Story Circles

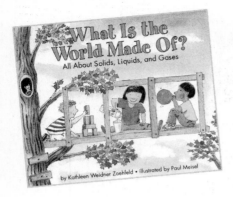

What Is the World Made Of?
All About Solids, Liquids, and Gases

by Kathleen Weidner Zoehfeld

❧❧❧

(HARPERCOLLINS, 1998)

"Have you ever seen anyone walk through a wall? Did you ever drink a glass of blocks? Have you ever played with a lemonade doll, or put on milk for socks?" The author asks intriguing questions as she delves into the concept of matter and its three states: solid, liquid, and gas. Speech bubbles add a touch of humor, while providing readers with additional information.

Before Reading

Preview the Text

Explain to students that this book tells about something called matter. Ask students what they think matter is. After students have a chance to respond, explain that matter is anything that takes up space and that it is usually found in three basic forms: solids (such as blocks, clothing, and books), liquids (such as water, juice, and milk), and gas (such as steam and the air we breathe). As you flip through the pages, invite students to share what they notice, including, for example, speech bubbles. Explain that authors use speech bubbles as a way to provide readers with additional information. (See page 34 for a related activity.)

Building Background Knowledge

Provide concrete examples of different types of matter: Pass a block around the circle. Ask questions such as "Does the block take up space?" "Does it change shape?" Explain that a block is a solid because it doesn't change shape unless it is altered in some way. Next, pass around a sealed plastic bag filled with water. Ask students if they think the water changes shape, and if it takes up space. Explain that water is a liquid that takes up space and can change shape. Finally, blow into an empty plastic bag and seal it. Pass the bag around the circle and ask if the air takes up space. Open the bag and let the air out, then ask students where the air went. Explain that the air spreads out to fill up any space that it is contained in, so the air (a gas) is in the room as you are speaking. Explain that all of the substances are forms of matter, in solid (block), liquid (water), and gas (air) form. Invite students to suggest other examples of each.

Teaching Tip

▲▲▲▲▲

Provide hands-on experiences with the properties of matter. Fill a sensory table with water and various containers, as well as items that will sink and float. Encourage children to explore the properties of water, and to discuss with classmates questions they have and discoveries they make. Periodically freshen the sensory table to include different substances, such as "oobleck" (see page 35).

Illustrations enhance readers' comprehension of nonfiction text. The illustrations in *What Is the World Made Of?* clearly show differences between the three types of matter. As you read, encourage children to use the illustrations to make better sense of the text. For example, when reading about the way temperature affects states of matter, point out the illustration of children playing in snow and ask: "Which state of matter is snow?" (*A snowman is solid, but when the snow melts it becomes a liquid.*)

After Reading

Encourage students to use the information in the book to classify items as solids, liquids, and gases.

1. In advance, make picture cards showing different types of matter (glue pictures from magazines or old workbooks to index cards).

2. Hold up each card, and have students identify the items in turn as a solid, liquid, or gas. Revisit text in the book to confirm their thinking.

Moving Molecules (Science, Movement)

This activity will help children understand how molecules move in solids, liquids, and gases. In advance, create a set of picture cards representing solids, liquids, and gases. Make one for each child. (You may use the pictures from Book Talk, above.)

1. Gather children in a circle and initiate a discussion about the different properties of solids, liquids, and gases. Explain that each type of matter is made up of different particles called molecules.

2. Give each child a card. Have all children with "solid" cards come to the center of the circle and create a formation that represents what the molecules in a solid look like: close together and still.

3. Gather children holding "liquid" cards, and have them behave as those molecules would: arranging themselves in the center but farther apart and moving slowly.

4. Finally, have children holding "gas" cards stand up and move about as molecules of a gas: rapidly and far apart from one another.

Teaching Tip

The Web site Rader's Chem4Kids (www.chem 4kids.com/files/matter _intro.html) is a useful resource for teachers who want to brush up on scientific concepts or for students yearning to learn more.

Book Links

It's Melting by Rozanne Lanczak Williams (Creative Teaching Press, 1994): Investigate things that melt, including snow, ice, and butter.

Let's Try It Out in the Water by Seymour Simon and Nicole Fauteux (Simon and Schuster, 2001): This activity-based book helps young scientists develop understanding of buoyancy, air pressure, and gravity.

Solid, Liquid or Gas? by Sally Hewitt (Children's Press, 1998): Observation-based activities invite exploration of solids, liquids, and gases.

Teaching Tip

To go further, provide copies of the speech bubble mini-book template (bottom of page 36). Let children use the pages to create their own nonfiction mini-books. They can write sentences to tell about their topic, draw pictures, and then complete the speech bubbles to tell more.

Temperature Controlled (Science)

Try these experiments to demonstrate the effect temperature has on solids, liquids, and gases. Revisit pages in the book to support students' understanding.

Experiment 1

1. Fill two glasses with water, one with hot, one with cold. Carefully set the glasses on a table and allow the water to settle a minute.

2. Place one drop of food coloring in each glass. Have children observe what happens. (Warm molecules move faster, so the food coloring in the hot water should have dispersed faster than the coloring in the cold water.)

Experiment 2

1. Blow up a balloon and measure its circumference. Place the balloon in a freezer for an hour or so.

2. Take the balloon out of the freezer and measure it again. What happened? (Colder temperatures make molecules stick closer together, therefore, they take up less space causing the balloon to shrink.)

Experiment 3

1. Fill a plastic bottle to the rim with water. Place the top on tightly. Place the bottle in a large plastic bag and seal.

2. Freeze the bottle overnight. Ask students to predict what they think will happen to the water in the bottle.

3. Remove the bottle and invite students to explain what they think happened. (Liquids increase in volume as they get cold, causing the bottle to expand and possibly crack. This is a good lesson in learning how to freeze liquids!)

Speech Bubble Writing (Language Arts)

Revisit pages in *What Is the World Made Of?* and direct students' attention to the speech bubbles. Explain that authors sometimes use speech bubbles to give readers extra information. Read and discuss the text in the speech bubbles. Then let students explore this text feature further by creating speech bubbles of their own.

1. Give each student a copy of the speech bubble template (top of page 36).

2. Revisit illustrations in the book that do not contain speech bubbles. Have students choose an illustration and create a speech bubble to go with it. For example, to go with the picture of two children throwing snowballs, a child might fill in the speech bubble to show the boy saying, "My snowball is a solid. Yours is, too!"

3. Use removable wall adhesive to affix children's speech bubbles to the corresponding pages. Read the pages with the new speech bubbles.

Investigating Oobleck (Science, Math, Language Arts)

In *Bartholomew and the Oobleck* by Dr. Seuss (Random House, 1949), the king is not satisfied with the everyday weather of sun, fog, rain, and snow and demands that something else fall from the sky. His page boy, Bartholomew, manages to have oobleck fall from the sky, and the kingdom then contends with the gummy substance that sticks to everything. Read aloud the book, and then extend students' understanding of matter with this hands-on activity.

1. Let students make their own oobleck by mixing two cups warm water with three cups cornstarch. Students will quickly find that oobleck is a mysterious substance; at times it feels like a solid, at other times it slips through their hands like a liquid.

2. Explain that the scientific term for *oobleck* is a mixture called colloidal suspension, in which particles of cornstarch are suspended, or float, in the water. Other substances known to be colloidal suspensions are milk, blood, and mud.

3. Make a reading-writing connection by inviting children to "add" a page to *What Is the World Make Of?* Give children copies of the speech bubble mini-book template (bottom of page 36). Have children write a sentence, draw a picture, and complete the speech bubble to share something they learned about oobleck.

Because students will encounter the words *solid*, *liquid*, and *gas* again and again throughout their school career, it is important to highlight these words as part of their vocabulary development. Let students share what they know about the terms. Revisit pages in the book that use these words and share the following definitions to add to their understanding as needed.

    solid: Matter that holds its shape. It often has a hard texture. Examples are rocks, wood, and metal.

    liquid: Matter that fills the shape of any container it is in. It has a feeling of wetness. Examples are water, syrup, and oil.

    gas: Matter that has no shape. It can fill a container of any size or shape. Examples are air and steam.

Play a game to reinforce understanding. Give each child three index cards on which you've written *solid*, *liquid*, *gas*. Call out the name of a substance, such as milk. Have students respond by holding up the appropriate card. Students will also enjoy calling out substances for classmates to identify.

Teaching Tip

Invite students to write a story about an imaginary substance that falls from the sky as oobleck did in *Bartholomew and the Oobleck*. Encourage children to be creative in naming their substance, and tell how the substance affected people in their story.

Keep in Mind...

Nonfiction texts do not always need to be read in their entirety. Sometimes it's appropriate to select portions of a text to support a topic of study. When reading portions of a text, share with children your reasons for that choice. Point out features of text that helped you find the portion you were looking for, such as headings, the table of contents, and the index. Be sure to model strategies you used, such as skimming and scanning, to choose the text selection.

Speech Bubble Templates

Speech Bubble Mini-Book

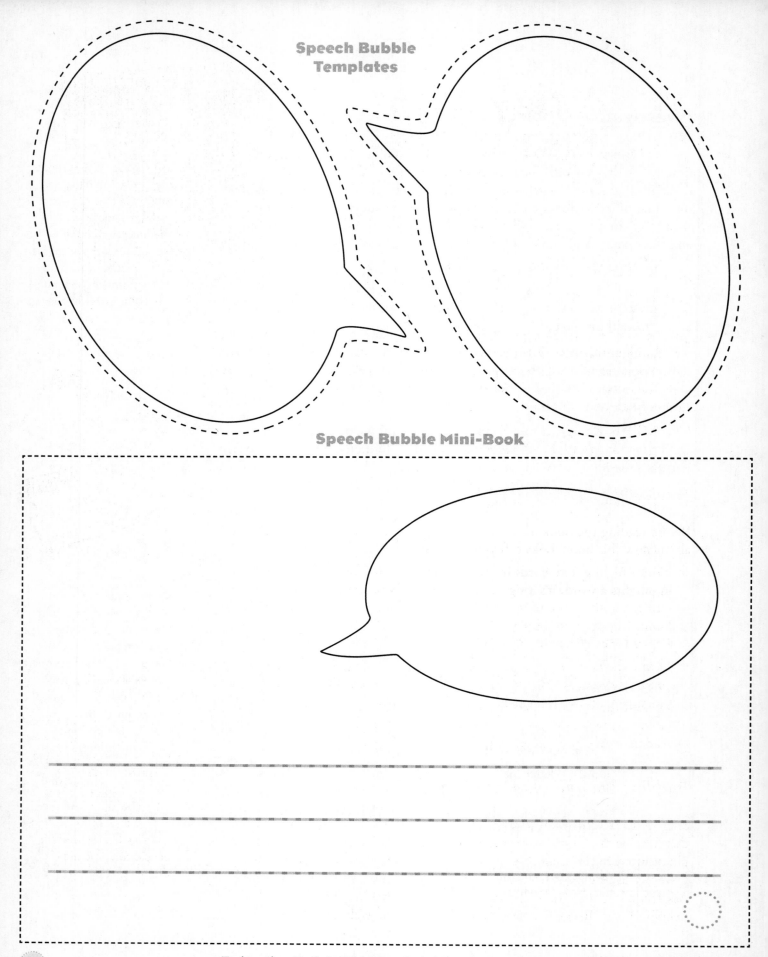

A Day With a Mail Carrier

by Jan Kottke

❧❧❧

(CHILDREN'S PRESS, 2000)

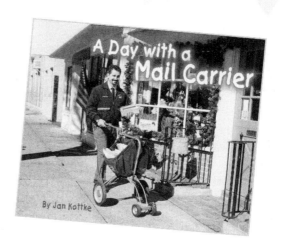

This book for young readers features a table of contents and an index, both important features of nonfiction text. Key words related to the topic of mail delivery are highlighted, inviting young readers to discover that this text feature signals important vocabulary. A New Words section at the end of the book offers further information.

Before Reading

Preview the Text

Before reading the book aloud, flip through the pages and guide a discussion about how this book looks different from storybooks children have read.

❋ Notice highlighted words in the text. Explain that when an author highlights a word, it's a sign to pay special attention to that word. Point out that authors often list and define highlighted words at the back of the book. Check the back of the book and notice the New Words section. Explain that *glossary* is another word for this feature.

❋ Locate the table of contents. Guide students to recognize that the table of contents shows how a nonfiction book is organized. It lists the big topics.

❋ Look at the index. Notice the alphabetical listing of topics. Let students choose a few and go to those page numbers. Explain that the index helps readers locate information quickly.

Building Background Knowledge

Share with students how you get your mail, and invite them to share how they receive mail. Does someone in their family drive to the post office to pick it up? Do they have it delivered to a mailbox at the end of their driveway or retrieve it from one of many boxes in an apartment complex? Ask students if they have ever seen mail carriers working in their neighborhood. Invite them to share what they know about this job.

Teaching Tip

▲▲▲▲▲

If you are able, visit a post office with children, or invite a mail carrier to the classroom to discuss his or her job. You might also take a neighborhood walk to locate collection stations (blue mailboxes where people can drop mail they're sending).

During Reading

As you read, make use of the pictures to teach comprehension strategies. Explicitly teaching comprehension strategies, such as inferring, improves children's comprehension. Pictures help readers to infer as they read. Have students identify what is happening in each picture and use what they see to make inferences, or construct new information. For example, ask:

✳ Why does Dominic have to get to the post office early? (*to sort the mail*)

✳ Why are some letters delivered directly to people? (*some letters are especially important*)

After Reading

Let students share what they learned about a mail carrier's job. Demonstrate how readers can use the table of contents and index to figure out where to locate information on these and other topics. Ask questions such as:

✳ How could you find information about loading the mail in this book?
✳ Which page is that on?
✳ Where can you find out how to have a letter picked up?

Point out that readers don't always read a nonfiction book from beginning to end—sometimes they use the contents page or index to decide where to begin reading.

Classroom Post Office (Language Arts, Social Studies, Math)

Set up a post office in your classroom for students to use. Encourage children to use the table of contents and index in *A Day With a Mail Carrier* to locate helpful information.

1. Have children make individual mailboxes by covering empty cereal boxes with construction paper and decorating as desired. Have them write their names on their mailboxes.

2. Stock the center with rubber stamps and stamp pads, stickers (to be used as stamps), envelopes, writing paper and utensils, cards, and materials to make cards.

3. Include some "junk mail" (check with the main office) for children to sort and "mail" to one another. Encourage children to write to one another and deliver the letters to the recipients' mailboxes.

The Letter Bear (Language Arts, Social Studies)

Children love to write letters! Here's an activity that will teach children how to use proper form when writing letters.

1. Give each child a copy of the reproducible bear-shaped letter template (page 41). Use the bear to review parts of a letter:

   ❋ Date   ❋ Body
   ❋ Salutation   ❋ Closing

2. Let children use the template to practice letter writing. Associating parts of the bear's body with parts of a letter will help children remember proper form.

3. To go further, let children choose a special person to correspond with, such as a grandparent or a friend (nearby or far away). Ask families to send in several envelopes that are stamped and addressed to their child's pen pal. Be sure each child who wants to write to someone has a pen pal. The school principal, nurse, librarian, and support staff may be happy to team up with students for this important activity. Have extra stamped envelopes on hand to use as needed.

Map My School (Math, Social Studies)

Mail carriers rely on maps to know where to deliver the mail. Map skills are also important for reading nonfiction text. Strengthen those skills with this collaborative activity.

1. After spending some time exploring maps, have children respond to these questions:

   ❋ What is a map?
   ❋ Why do people use maps?
   ❋ What do maps show?
   ❋ How would a map be helpful to a mail carrier?

2. Have students pretend that a mail carrier has to deliver mail to each classroom in your school (or a wing of the school, if the building is large). Invite students to cooperatively draw a map to help the mail carrier locate each room. To make this more manageable, you might have students work on this in small groups, each responsible for a different section. Encourage students to label places on their map and make a key to show what different symbols mean.

Teaching Tip

In preparation for creating a map of their school, share *Me on the Map* by Joan Sweeney (Crown Publishers, 1996). Invite children to notice how maps use colors, lines, shapes, and symbols to represent places, and to use the same elements as they create their map.

What Are Those Words? (Language Arts)

Young readers often wonder about pronunciation keys: What are these words and why do they look this way? Use the New Words page in the back of *A Day With a Mail Carrier* to introduce this text feature and help children understand how pronunciation keys help readers better understand the text.

1. Use an overhead to display the New Words page. Point out the words (in blue) and ask: "If you were going to sound out this word, how do you think you would say it?"

2. Point out the parentheses next to each word, and explain that what's inside tells readers how to say the word. Let students tell what they notice about the pronunciation keys—for example, the use of boldfaced type and hyphens.

3. Model how to use a pronunciation key to sound out a word. Explain that being able to pronounce what seems like an unknown word sometimes helps readers recognize it and know its meaning.

4. Mask words on the New Words list and let students take turns using the pronunciation keys to identify the words. Unmask the words to check their guesses.

Keep in Mind...

▲▲▲▲▲▲

Scaffolding is very important when introducing a new book to young readers. Try some of these strategies when using books for guided reading.

● Introduce the topic of the book.

● Encourage conversation among children about the book.

● Share what you know about the topic.

● Point out the features of the nonfiction text.

● Encourage students to notice print features, such as where to start reading, directionality of print, and punctuation.

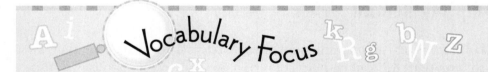

Vocabulary Focus

Revisit highlighted words in the book, and list them on chart paper: *doorbell, load, mailbox, mail carrier, mail cart, post office.* Read the words aloud, and have students read them with you. Deepen children's word knowledge with the following activities.

◆ Invite students to supply a definition for each word. Then read aloud from the New Words list at the back of the book and have students check their understanding. Let students revise their definitions as needed.

◆ Play a matching game to help students add the words to their vocabulary "banks." Start by calling out a word, such as *mail carrier.* Challenge students to find a word that matches in some way—for example, *mail carrier, doorbell,* and *post office* all have double letters. Repeat to review features of other words—for example, "I see a word that rhymes with *toad.* What is it?" (*load*)

(Date) _____

(Salutation) **Dear** _____,

The Letter Bear

(Body) _____

_____

_____

_____

_____

_____

_____

(Closing) **Sincerely,**

_____

Giving Thanks
The 1621 Harvest Feast

by Kate Waters

(SCHOLASTIC, 2000)

Step right into the year 1621 and join the Wampanoag people and the English settlers in their harvest feast. Stunning photographs of this reenactment will make students feel they are a part of this historical event. Endnotes clear up misconceptions about the first Thanksgiving, and a glossary helps readers understand Old English and Wampanoag words.

Before Reading

Preview the Text

While paging through the book with students, call attention to the format of the text, which tells the story from the viewpoint of two young boys: a Wampanoag and an English settler. Explain that each boy is explaining the feast from his own experience. (Follow up on text structure with During Reading, page 43.)

Building Background Knowledge

Invite children to share what they know about Thanksgiving and the first Thanksgiving feast. Together, locate Plymouth, Massachusetts, and England on a globe. Trace the route that the pilgrims sailed on the Mayflower to come to the "New World." Enhance students' knowledge as needed with the following facts.

* The pilgrims left England so they could have religious freedom.
* Tisquantum (Squanto) helped the pilgrims learn how to grow native plants.
* The Wampanoag people give thanks every day. They do not have one special day set aside for Thanksgiving. The pilgrims occasionally set aside a day to give thanks, but these days were for prayers, not for feasting.
* Massasoit, the *sachem* ("king") of the Pokanoket village, visited the pilgrims during their harvest feast; however, historians do not believe this was a planned event.

While reading this book, explain that it is important to make a distinction between the two storytellers, and that there are text features that help readers do so.

1. Point out the red and blue headings on different pages. Explain that headings help readers predict what comes next in the text. Resolved White's story is headed with red text, and Dancing Moccasins's story is headed with blue text.

2. As you read, make a distinction between the two boys by pointing to each boy, or by changing your voice to represent the different characters.

3. Occasionally, pause at the red or blue heading and ask students which boy is going to be "speaking." If students are not sure, model how to revisit text, in this case the headings, to figure it out.

After Reading

After reading, have students respond to the book with a quick-write (or -draw) about something that surprised them. The quick-write should take no more than five to ten minutes to complete; it is used as a way for students to quickly record their ideas. Other quick-write prompts include:

* What part of the book left you with more questions?
* Describe how you think one of the boys in the book may feel.
* What did this book make you think about?

Compare and Contrast (Language Arts, Social Studies)

Authors of nonfiction text sometimes use comparisons to organize information. This text structure helps readers understand what is the same and what is different. Discuss with students how *Giving Thanks* is organized. Guide them to understand that by alternating between the stories of the two boys, the author helps readers learn how they are alike and different.

1. Draw a Venn diagram on chart paper. Label the left side "Dancing Moccasins" and the right side "Resolved White."

2. Reread portions of *Giving Thanks*. As you read, pause to let children identify similarities and differences in the lives of the two boys.

3. Record observations on the Venn diagram. Guide students to understand how this graphic organizer helps them visualize similarities

(continues)

Teaching Tip

Remind students to look for headings when they read, and to use these key words as a strategy to predict what will come next.

Keep in Mind...

Quick-writes (or -draws) are a powerful way for children to keep track of their learning. Children can keep these pieces together in a notebook or binder and look back on them to review what they have learned, and to note growth in their responses. These entries are also useful as springboards for discussions about nonfiction topics.

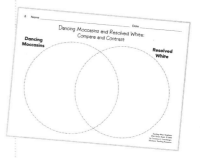

The conditions on the Mayflower were cramped and uncomfortable. To help children understand what it might have been like to be a passenger on this journey, mark off a 68- by 22-foot area on the playground or in the gym, the dimensions of the living space on the Mayflower. Have students stand in the "Mayflower," and add children and teachers from other classes until you have about 130 people. Remind students that the pilgrims traveled 2,750 miles for 65 days on this ship, living their daily lives in this space!

and differences. Point out that the information in the overlapping area shows how the boys' lives are similar. The information outside of this area represents how their lives are different.

4. Give each student a Venn diagram template (page 46). Continue to read portions of the book, pausing to let children add information to their Venn diagram. Conclude by inviting children to share their comparisons. Add new information to the class Venn diagram.

Squanto's Secret   (Science, Language Arts)

Tisquantum (also called Squanto) was a neighbor to the English colonists. He spoke English and helped the colonists to plant native crops. Some say he taught the early settlers to plant a fish as fertilizer with each corn seed. Try this activity to compare and contrast seeds planted with and without fertilizer.

1. Have children plant several corn seeds in each of two cups of soil. Keep the contents of each moist, but to one add fertilizer, such as Squanto's Secret™ (a fish-based fertilizer available at many garden stores).

2. Have students record their observations on a sheet of paper divided into two sections. Have them label one side "No Fertilizer" and the other "Fertilizer." (As in the book, they can use a different color for each heading.) Discuss results and encourage students to draw conclusions.

Thanksgiving Myths Uncovered   (Language Arts)

There are many myths about the English settlers' first Thanksgiving in America. Use this activity to clarify such misconceptions and give children a chance to try out some features of nonfiction in their own writing.

1. After reading *Giving Thanks*, ask students if they learned something different about the first Thanksgiving than what they originally thought. Revisit the book's endnotes to bring more misconceptions to the surface and to reinforce students' awareness of this feature of nonfiction. Explain that a myth is something that is widely believed but is found to be fictitious.

2. Make a class-generated list of Thanksgiving myths. Have students choose one myth to write about, explaining both the myth and the truth. Have students use the book as a model for their writing, highlighting in one color the heading "The Myth," and in a different color the heading "The Truth."

Pumpkin Play Clay (Math)

During pilgrim times, pumpkins were called *pompions*. Locate this word in the glossary, and then have fun making pumpkin, or *pompion*, play clay. Place it in the dramatic play center with pans, bowls, and utensils and encourage students to role-play their own first harvest feast. It's always a great hit because it smells like pumpkin pie!

1. Mix the first five ingredients (see right) in a large saucepan. Stir constantly over medium heat (adult only) until mixed well, about 15 minutes.

2. When cool, knead in food coloring and pumpkin spice. Store in a covered plastic container or reclosable bag. Use the play clay recipe to make a connection to this form of nonfiction. Revisit the recipe for Hominy Grits at the back of *Giving Thanks* to provide another example.

Pumpkin Play Clay

- 3 cups water
- 3 cups flour
- 3 tablespoons vegetable oil
- 3 tablespoons cream of tartar
- $1\frac{1}{2}$ cups salt
- orange food coloring
- $1\frac{1}{2}$ tablespoons pumpkin spice

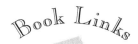

Book Links

On the Mayflower: Voyage of the Ship's Apprentice and a Passenger Girl by Kate Waters (Scholastic, 1996): Outstanding photographs bring to life this realistic account of the voyage of the Mayflower.

Pilgrims of Plymouth by Susan E. Goodman (National Geographic, 1999): Photos taken at Plimoth Plantation support simple text to explain the days of the pilgrims.

Tapenum's Day: A Wampanoag Indian Boy in Pilgrim Times by Kate Waters (Scholastic, 1996): Photographs and text tell the story of a young Wampanoag boy in the 1620s. Other books in the series include ***Samuel Eaton's Day: A Day in the Life of a Pilgrim Boy*** and ***Sarah Morton's Day: A Day in the Life of a Pilgrim Girl***.

Vocabulary Focus

Resolved White speaks in a seventeenth-century English dialect, so some of what he says sounds unfamiliar to our modern-day ears. Use these words as the basis for a mini-lesson on glossaries, an important feature of nonfiction text.

1. Revisit passages that contain the following words: *pompion* (a squash or pumpkin), *samp* (porridge or soup made with corn), and *venison* (meat of a deer). Let students tell what they think each word means.

2. Locate each word in the glossary and read the definition. Use the following questions to explore this important text feature.

   ◆ Which word is first? [Last?] What letter does this word start with?

   ◆ What do you notice about the way the words are organized? (*They're in alphabetical order.*)

   ◆ How do you think a glossary helps readers quickly locate definitions of unfamiliar words? (*If a word begins with a letter at the end of the alphabet, for example, readers know to go right to the end of the glossary. They don't have to read every word.*)

   ◆ Why is using a glossary to look up a word when reading easier than using a dictionary? (*A glossary is just a page or two; a dictionary is much bigger.*)

3. As an extension, let students pair up to locate and explore glossaries in classroom books. (Remind them that glossaries are located in the back.)

Teaching Tip

Audio clips at the Web site Plimoth Plantation (www.plimoth.org) allow children to hear the way the English settlers spoke.

45

Dancing Moccasins and Resolved White:
Compare and Contrast

Resolved White

Dancing Moccasins

Teaching About Nonfiction With Picture Books © 2008 by Constance J. Leuenberger, Scholastic Teaching Resources

Martin's Big Words
The Life of Dr. Martin Luther King, Jr.

by Doreen Rappaport

(HYPERION, 2001)

When Dr. King was a child, he said, "When I grow up I'm going to get big words, too." This Caldecott Honor pictorial biography of Dr. Martin Luther King Jr.'s life is told through rich collage artwork and reverent text. The text is interspersed with other quotes from this great civil rights leader. Endnotes provide a timeline of important dates in Dr. King's life.

Before Reading

Preview the Text

Share the book's cover with students, and ask them if they know who is pictured. To fill in any gaps students might have, explain that the man pictured is Dr. Martin Luther King Jr. Share a little of his life, and then preview the text with students, noticing the use of quotation marks.

1. Point out words in quotations (they are also printed in a bright color, making them stand out on the page).

2. Explain that quotations are used to indicate that someone is speaking. Invite students to guess who they think is speaking the words in quotations.

3. Ask students if they think that some of the words used in the quotations are "big words." Point out the link between these words and the title of the book.

Building Background Knowledge

Invite students to share what they know about Dr. Martin Luther King Jr.

1. Use a map to locate Montgomery, Alabama, and Memphis, Tennessee. Explain that these two cities were important in the civil rights movement, Montgomery for the bus boycotts and Memphis because it was where Dr. King was assassinated.

2. Point out that many African Americans in the south were oppressed, and did not have the rights that most other people had at the time. Share examples.

3. Explain that this book is a biography and follows Dr. King through his life from a young boy to the time of his death.

Keep in Mind...

Visualizing helps children to hold on to information, and makes reading more interesting. While reading *Martin's Big Words*, encourage children to "play movies in their head." As students' reading becomes more sophisticated, visualizing is a skill that will help them be better able to stick with more difficult texts.

Teaching Tip

▲▲▲▲▲▲▲

Enhance your study of
Martin Luther King, Jr. by
accessing audio clips of his
speeches at The King Center
(www.thekingcenter.org).

During Reading

As you read, guide children in paying close attention to the text structure (time order).

1. Have students compare Dr. King's age at the beginning of the book with his age at the end.

2. Point out the Important Dates page at the back of the book, which outlines Dr. King's life according to key events.

3. Explain that biographies often tell the story of a person's life chronologically. Chronological or time order often makes the most sense in biographies because it explains a person's life from beginning to end.

After Reading

 Book Talk This is a very powerful book, with intense use of language. After reading, invite students to share how the book made them feel. Guide their discussion with these prompts.

✳ What part of the book was most meaningful for you?

✳ What quote from Martin Luther King, Jr. would you like to remember?

✳ Let students respond to the quote "Sooner or later, all the people of the world will have to discover a way to live together."

381 Days (Math, Language Arts, Social Studies)

"For 381 days they walked to work and school and church. They walked in rain and cold and in blistering heat." Revisit this passage from *Martin's Big Words* about the Montgomery bus boycott. Point out that numbers in nonfiction text often signal important information. Discuss the significance of the number 381 in the text. Then use a hands-on experience to deepen understanding.

1. Invite students to share how different modes of transportation help them get from place to place each day. Ask: "What it would be like if you could no longer use that transportation?"

2. Use a calendar to count up the 381 days. Note with students how many months it took to count this high (more than 12).

3. Initiate a discussion about how students could represent the number 381 with tangible objects—for example, by counting out 381 paper clips, pennies, or other small objects.

4. Choose an item and lay each of the 381 pieces end to end. Have students imagine walking everywhere for that many days, in all kinds of weather and for long distances, in order to peacefully make a point.

"Martin Said 'Love' When Others Said 'Hate'"

(Language Arts, Social Studies)

Readers of *Martin's Big Words* learn that "Martin said 'love' when others said 'hate.' He said 'together' when others said 'separate.' He said 'peace' when others said 'war.'" Using these words as a springboard, guide students in making connections between Dr. King's dreams and their own lives.

1. Give each child a copy of the chart (page 51). Read the first word in column 1 (*hate*). Have children write in column 2 what they might say instead, using what they know about Dr. King as inspiration.

2. Have children continue to complete the chart, reading the words in column 1 and writing their words (or those they think Dr. King might have chosen) in column 2.

Walking in His Footsteps (Language Arts, Social Studies)

This activity makes an inspirational bulletin board that will motivate students to set and achieve meaningful goals.

1. Have students trace one of their feet and cut out the tracing.

2. Inside the tracing, have students write one thing they can do to carry out Dr. King's dream.

3. Display footprints on a bulletin board with the title "Walking in His Footsteps." Encourage students to add information they learn to the display to educate others about Dr. King and his work.

My Own Timeline (Language Arts, Math, Social Studies)

Using the Important Dates list at the end of *Martin's Big Words* as a model, invite students to create timelines of their own lives to learn more about this feature of nonfiction.

1. Let students use what they know about the words *time* and *line* to explain what a timeline is. Timelines are a type of diagram or graphic aid that use chronological order to show a series of events. They show a lot of information in a relatively small space, and are visually easy to follow. Timelines also help readers understand how events are related.

2. Revisit and discuss the timeline in *Martin's Big Words*. Guide children to notice how the dates are arranged from earlier to later.

3. As homework, have students make a list of important events from their life (all or part of it). Send a note home with the assignment, inviting families to help.

(continues)

Happy Birthday, Martin Luther King by Jean Marzollo (Scholastic, 1992): This gentle account highlights aspects of Dr. King's life that children will find most meaningful.

Martin Luther King Jr. by Pamela Walker (Children's Press, 2001): A table of contents, list of new words, index, and photographs make this a perfect nonfiction choice for young learners.

Martin Luther King, Jr.: A Photographic Story of a Life by Amy Pastan (Dorling Kindersley, 2004): Color photographs tell the story of Dr. King, with sidebars that explain nonviolent resistance and grassroots movements.

4. In class, have students make a timeline, complete with illustrations and a title. Discuss with children their timelines, asking questions to guide understanding:

   ✳ What is this timeline about?
   ✳ What year does your timeline begin?
   ✳ What year does it end?
   ✳ How many years are covered in your timeline (elapsed time)?
   ✳ What can someone learn from this timeline?

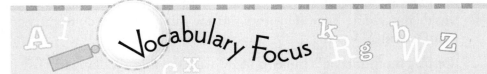

Children may be unfamiliar with vocabulary relating to the civil rights movement. Help them make connections by comparing words.

1. Reread portions of the text with the following words. Give children a chance to use context to figure out the meaning.

   protest: To strongly disagree with something.

   segregation: To keep certain groups of people apart—for example, by making them go to different schools, live in different areas, and use different public services such as buses, restaurants, and water fountains.

2. Write the words on chart paper and model their pronunciation. Let students say the words with you.

3. Encourage a deeper understanding of the vocabulary by having students compare and contrast the words with others. For example, ask: What words have a similar meaning to *protest*? (*object, be against, oppose*) What words have an opposite meaning? (*agree, approve, be for*) Guide students to a clearer understanding of *segregation* by discussing words they may know. For example, a familiar classroom expectation may be the idea of *including* others (or, "You can't say, 'You can't play'"). Discuss how this word relates to *segregation*.

"Martin Said 'Love' When Others Said 'Hate'"

Others Might Say...	I Can Say...
Hate	
Separate	
War	
No	
Stop	
Wait	
Fear	
Refuse	

Snowflake Bentley

by Jacqueline Briggs Martin

(HOUGHTON MIFFLIN, 1998)

"In the days when farmers worked with ox and sled and cut the dark with lantern light, there lived a boy who loved snow more than anything else in the world." This Caldecott award-winning book strikes a perfect balance between nonfiction features and the quintessential beauty of picture books. Information-packed sidebars cozy up to charming woodcut illustrations, making this a treat that children will return to again and again.

Before Reading

Preview the Text

While looking through the pages with students, point out the sidebars located on most of the pages.

❋ Ask children if they know why the sidebars are there.

❋ Do they think the sidebars are part of the story of Snowflake Bentley's life, or do they think they give some other information?

❋ Explain that sidebars give readers information that enhances the book, but that they are not always part of the main story.

Building Background Knowledge

Explain that Snowflake Bentley lived in Jericho, Vermont. Together, locate Vermont on a map. Identify Vermont as a place that gets a lot of snow in the winter. (Students can find out just how much with So Much Snow!, page 53.) Invite children to share what they know about snow and snowflakes. Ask:

❋ Have you ever played in snow?

❋ What kinds of things can you do in snow? (*shovel, sled, make snowmen, ski*)

❋ Have you ever seen a snowflake up close? What do you notice about snowflakes?

Teaching Tip

▲▲▲▲▲

For children who have never seen snow, have pictures available.

During Reading

As you read, be sure to share the informational sidebar boxes. Notice how these relate to the story, and point to the boxes as you read them so students can differentiate between the main text and this feature.

After Reading

Book Talk

Invite students to compare and contrast the information given in the main text of the book with the information given in the sidebars. Ask:

✳ Why do you think the sidebars are important?

✳ How is the information in the sidebars different from the main part of the book? Why is each important?

✳ How do the sidebars make it easy to locate important facts quickly?

✳ What part of this book was most interesting to you? Why?

So Much Snow! (Math)

Tell students that the average snowfall in Jericho, Vermont, is 120 inches a year. Note that it's easy to see why Snowflake Bentley became so interested in snow!

1. Together, research the average total snowfall in your area and compare that with the average snowfall in Jericho. Explain that all the snow does not fall at the same time, but if it did, it would be 120 inches high!

2. Give pairs of students a ball of yarn or string, a measuring tool, and scissors. Have partners measure and cut a 120-inch length of yarn.

3. Tape the strings from the floor up on a classroom wall (if tall enough), or to the building outside, and invite students to envision that much snow! Engage children in a discussion about other things that are 120 inches tall, such as two people standing on top of each other, or a tree.

4. Finally, invite students to write about (or draw pictures of) what they would do if they had 120 inches of snow to play in.

Snowflake Bentley Mini-Book

(Science, Social Studies, Language Arts)

Many nonfiction books feature sidebars. Use this activity to provide practice in recognizing this text feature and to give students an opportunity to try out sidebars in their own writing.

1. Revisit sidebars in *Snowflake Bentley* and other nonfiction books. Have students identify physical features of sidebars—for example, they are often enclosed in a box, they are set to the side of the main text, and they usually have their own headings.

(continues)

Teaching Tip

Visit an online gallery of Snowflake Bentley's work at www.snowflakebentley.com. For movies of snowflakes growing, go to www.its .caltech.edu/~atomic/ snowcrystals).

2. Give each student four sheets of paper and a copy of the mini-book sidebar boxes and sentence strips (page 56). Have students cut apart the sidebar boxes and sentence strips and glue matching sets (sidebar and sentence strip) on their paper (see sample, left). Show children how to use the snowflakes in the top corner of each sidebar box and sentence strip to match them up.

3. Review with students how to complete the mini-book, drawing a picture to go with each sentence strip and filling in three facts for each sidebar.

4. When their pages are finished, have students create a cover, then place pages in order and staple to bind.

5. Invite children to share their books, and notice the many ways they found to complete the sidebars and illustrate the text.

Crystal Formations (Science)

This science experiment is a great way for students to see how crystals, such as snowflakes, form.

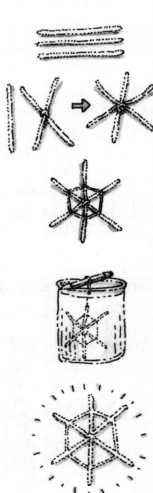

1. Cut a white pipe cleaner into three equal sections. Twist the three pieces of pipe cleaner together to make a six-pointed form.

2. Tie string from point to point around the pipe cleaners to make it resemble a snowflake. Tie a string to the top of the pipe cleaner form, and tie the other end of the string to a pencil.

3. Fill a clear, wide-mouth jar with boiling water. Caution: Warm up the jar in advance so it won't break. Keep children at a safe distance.

4. Add three tablespoons Borax for each cup of water. Stir until dissolved. Add a few drops of blue food coloring if you wish.

5. Submerse the pipe cleaner flake in the solution, laying the pencil across the top of the jar to keep the string from falling in.

6. Allow the snowflake to soak overnight. The next day you will find a crystal! Invite students to observe the crystal as a "scientist" would, and then draw and label what they see.

Six-Sided Snowflakes (Art, Math, Language Arts, Social Studies)

These snowflakes offer a twist on the standard paper snowflakes. Follow the steps below to make beautiful six-sided snowflakes. When children are finished, they can glue their snowflakes to dark construction paper. Have them write one fact about Snowflake Bentley on a strip of plain paper and glue it beneath the snowflake. These make an inviting bulletin board display to complement a study of Snowflake Bentley.

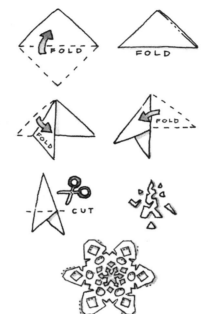

1. Fold an $8\frac{1}{2}$-inch-square sheet of paper to form a triangle. Fold again to form a smaller triangle.

2. Measure in $1\frac{3}{4}$ inches from one point of the triangle and fold in. Repeat for the opposite corner.

3. Cut off the ends of these two points (straight across).

4. Snip pieces from each side of the triangle. Open to reveal a six-sided snowflake.

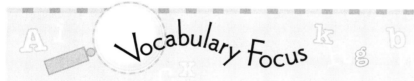

Vocabulary Focus

Explore content-area words from *Snowflake Bentley* with a seasonal word wall.

1. Revisit pages in the book with the following words. Invite students to say the words with you and explain what they mean.

   crystal: A solid that has a geometrically arranged pattern (as in a snowflake).

   moisture: Wetness.

   snowbelt: An area where a large amount of snow falls.

2. Make a word wall to gather words that describe and relate to each season, beginning with winter, so students can make connections to the book. Other words for winter might include: *snow, snowflake, icicle, frost, blizzard, freezing, snow showers,* and *snow day.* As a visual aid, provide seasonal shapes for each word wall—such as a snowflake for winter, a flower for spring, a sun for summer, and a leaf for fall.

3. Use the word wall for vocabulary-building games (for example, matching definitions with words or matching words with features such as double letters) and as a resource for students' writing.

Book Links

Snow Crystals by W. A. Bentley and W. J. Humphreys (Dover Publications, 1962): Take a look at more than 2,000 of Bentley's snowflake photographs.

The Snowflake: A Water Cycle Story by Neil Waldman (Millbrook Press, 2003): Follow a snowflake through the water cycle, from earth to cloud and back again.

The Snowflake: Winter's Secret Beauty by Kenneth Libbrecht (Voyageur Press, 2003): Stunning photographs of snowflakes are combined with easy-to-read, informative text.

Keep in Mind...

Snowflake Bentley is a type of literature termed "multigenre" because it melds together aspects of picture books, such as the beautiful woodcut illustrations, with features of nonfiction books. Bentley's biography is told in story form with informational sidebars, which weave together aspects of both fiction and nonfiction. Using multigenre books in the classroom is a natural way to teach across the disciplines.

Snowflake Bentley as a Boy

Three facts about Snowflake Bentley's childhood:

1. _____

_____

2. _____

_____

3. _____

_____

①

Snowflake Bentley the Photographer

Three facts about how Snowflake Bentley took photos:

1. _____

_____

2. _____

_____

3. _____

_____

②

Get to Know Snow!

Three facts about snowflakes:

1. _____

_____

2. _____

_____

3. _____

_____

③

Snowflake Bentley learned a lot about snowflakes.

Snowflake Bentley took photos of snowflakes.

Snowflake Bentley liked snowstorms.

This Land Is Your Land

by Woody Guthrie

(LITTLE, BROWN, 1998)

From California to the New York island, this informative picture book teaches about United States history and geography. This book includes all of Woody Guthrie's original lyrics of the song, including some that were omitted in his 1949 version. Oil paintings depict landmarks throughout the U.S. and important events in our nation's history. The last section offers a tribute to Woody Guthrie written by Pete Seeger, and a biography of Woody's life, complete with black and white photos.

Before Reading

Preview the Text

As you look at the pages with children, point out the print on many of the pages that features lyrics and quotes from Guthrie. Notice the landmarks that are depicted in the art. Share the photos of Woody Guthrie at the end of the book and explain that he was a famous folksinger who championed the rights of the common person.

Building Background Knowledge

Woody Guthrie wrote this song in response to the Great Depression and the Dust Bowl, both of which may be difficult for children to understand. As sensitively as possible, try to help students understand some of the issues surrounding these events. Begin by locating Kansas, Oklahoma, Texas, Colorado, and New Mexico. Explain that in the 1930s there was a severe drought (a period of no rain) in these areas of the United States. This area became known as the Dust Bowl. Share related information (provided in the back of the book).

During Reading

This book of lyrics lends itself to repeated readings in several different ways. For the first reading, recite only the lyrics. In subsequent readings, invite students to look carefully at the illustrations as you read about the America of the 1930s. Later, invite students to sing along as you read Woody's lyrics the way they were meant to be read, in song.

Teaching Tip

If possible, before reading the text, play a recording of Guthrie singing "This Land Is Your Land." Students may recognize the tune, which will help them make connections to the book. Let students locate the places mentioned in the first verse ("from California, to the New York island, from the redwood forest, to the gulf stream waters...").

Book Talk

Encourage children to share how this book and the song make them feel. Are they able to visualize Woody Guthrie walking through each place in the United States? Invite students to study the remarkable illustrations and all the information that is packed into each page. How does the art help them understand the text? Have students make connections to information you shared earlier. (See Building Background Knowledge, page 57.) Leave the book out for students to peruse on their own and experience its full impact.

Class Big Book   (Language Arts, Art)

Woody's song brings many different images to mind. Invite children to document their own images with this activity.

1. On chart paper, write the words to "This Land Is Your Land," following the format of the book by Guthrie and Jakobsen. Be sure to write the words at the bottom of each page, leaving the bulk of the area free for illustrations.

2. Invite students to think of places in the United States they would like to illustrate on each page of the class book.

3. Divide the class into groups by interest and have each group illustrate a page. Read the completed book together. Share it with other classes.

From California to the New York Island
(Social Studies, Art)

Strengthen students' art and map skills with this fun activity.

1. Share the foldout map in the book with students. Have students tell why they think the author included a map in this book. Explain that maps use lines, shapes, symbols, and colors to represent places. Maps are useful for showing a large place, such as the U.S., in a small space.

2. Compare and contrast different maps with the map in the book. Initiate a discussion with students about the pictures on the map. What do the pictures tell readers?

3. Give each child an enlarged copy of the reproducible map (page 60). Review the function of the inset on the map. You might locate Hawaii and Alaska on a map that shows their actual geographic position. Invite students to use the map in the book as inspiration to create their own maps that reflect the song "This Land Is Your Land." Provide books and other materials about states and landmarks as reference.

Keep in Mind...

Studies have shown that most of adult reading is nonfiction. Maps are one example of the nonfiction reading we do. Look for opportunities in daily instruction to point out and teach different types of maps. For example, use transportation maps of your community or state to show how maps can help people get from one place to another. Other examples include political maps (show information such as countries, states, and cities), physical maps (show mountains, rivers, oceans, and other features of Earth), and landform maps (use colors and symbols to show Earth's landmasses and bodies of water).

"Stick Up for What You Know Is Right" (Social Studies)

Invite students to get to know Woody Guthrie a little better by exploring one of his favorite sayings: "Stick up for what you know is right."

1. Discuss what Woody Guthrie meant when he said, "Stick up for what you know is right." Share that he was an advocate for the poor and underprivileged, and in this way he was sticking up for what was right.

2. Invite students to share what they "know is right"—for example, "It's important to treat others the way you want to be treated." Have children work with partners to create a poster that illustrates Guthrie's words. Display posters in the school community to inspire others to join in to make the world a better place.

Informational Study Groups (Social Studies, Language Arts, Art)

This Land Is Your Land offers many springboards for content area study.

1. After reading the book, students may want to learn more about Woody Guthrie, folksingers, the 1930s, or certain areas of the United States. Form informational study groups based on students' interests. Gather materials to help each group learn more about the selected topic.

2. Invite students to share presentations about their topic. This is an excellent opportunity to allow choices that support preferred modes of learning.

Book Links

Bling Blang by Woody Guthrie (Candlewick, 2000): Fun-loving illustrations bring this toe-tapping Woody tune to life.

New Baby Train by Woody Guthrie (Little, Brown, 2004): Marla Frazee's illustrations depict new babies riding into town on a train and being delivered to welcoming households.

Woody Guthrie: Poet of the People by Bonnie Christensen (Knopf, 2001): Powerful illustrations and lyrical text tell a biography of Woody Guthrie.

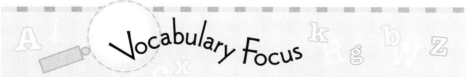

Vocabulary Focus

This Land Is Your Land may introduce some unfamiliar terms to students. Here are two you may want to take a closer look at.

relief office: During the Great Depression, this was a place people in need could go to get food, clothing, and shelter.

trespassing: To go onto somebody's land or property without permission.

Revisit pages of the book that use these words, and have students use the text and illustrations to figure out what the words might mean. Encourage students to relate the words to what they know. For example, baseball fans might know that a *relief* pitcher relieves or helps out a pitcher who is injured or can't continue for some reason. Students may recall having seen a "No Trespassing" sign and understand that it means "keep out."

Name _____

Date _____

From California to the New York Island

Atlantic Ocean

Gulf of Mexico

Pacific Ocean

Alaska

Hawaii

Wake Up, World!
A Day in the Life of Children Around the World

by Beatrice Hollyer

(HENRY HOLT, 1999)

Captioned photographs take readers through a typical day in the lives of eight children from around the world. A large map at the beginning of the book locates each child's country, including the United Kingdom, the United States of America, Brazil, Ghana, India, Australia, Vietnam, and Russia.

Before Reading

Preview the Text

Overviewing is a way to preview a text with scanning and skimming. This is a helpful strategy for reading nonfiction texts as it helps readers identify how the text is organized and get ready to read. Take a moment to overview the text with students. Invite them to notice the following features:

❋ The layout of the book, and placement of photographs and text

❋ Headings

❋ Graphic aids, such as the world map

❋ Diagrams locating where each child lives

❋ Highlighted text (children's names and their countries are in uppercase letters)

❋ A different graphic following each child through the book, making it easy for readers to organize information as they read

Building Background Knowledge

The focus of this book is on creating awareness of the ways in which children around the world are similar. Details in their lives may be different, but children everywhere wake up, get dressed, learn, and play. Use a globe to spark a discussion about the topic.

❋ Look at a globe with students. As you rotate the globe, wonder aloud about how children around the world live, work, and play. Elicit from students how they think their lives might be similar or different.

❋ Discuss how factors such as weather, economy, and customs might play a part in the way people live in different regions of the world.

Teaching Tip

▲ ▲ ▲ ▲ ▲

To help students understand different cultures better, set up a multicultural center in your classroom. Gather and display photos of people from around the world, as well as flags from different countries. Display nonfiction and fiction picture books about different cultures.

Book Links

Children Around the World by Donata Montanari (Kids Can Press, 2001): Readers meet children from 12 different countries and learn about their homes, food, schools, and families.

Houses and Homes (Around the World series) by Ann Morris (Lothrop, Lee and Shepard, 1992): Striking photos give readers a peek into how people around the world live.

Throw Your Tooth on the Roof: Tooth Traditions From Around the World by Selby Beeler (Houghton Mifflin, 1998): This playful book takes a look at traditions children around the world have regarding losing their teeth.

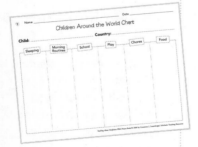

During Reading

This book is full of information that needs to be synthesized while reading. The use of graphics helps readers organize that information.

1. As you read, point out the graphic that represents each child (for example, the snowflake for Sashsa). Think aloud about how this visual aid helps you organize your thinking and keep track of information.

2. Let children take turns using the graphics to identify which child you are reading about.

After Reading

Invite children's responses to the text with these questions.

* What surprised you about this book? What did you learn about a different culture that you didn't already know?

* After reading this book, what would you like to know more about?

* What are some ways in which you are similar to the children in this book?

* What do you think would surprise [name child from the book] about the children in our class?

Children Around the World Chart

(Social Studies, Language Arts)

Like other nonfiction texts, *Wake Up, World!* contains a lot of information. Using a graphic organizer can help students make sense of the way text is organized and better understand what they read.

1. Explain to students that when nonfiction books have a lot of information, it is helpful to organize the material in a way that is easy to understand.

2. Give each student a copy of the reproducible chart (page 64; enlarge first). Divide the class into eight groups. Assign each group a child from the book. Have children fill in the child's name and country at the top of the chart. As you reread the book, have students record information on the chart. Be sure students understand that this is a form of note taking, and they need not include every detail from the book on the chart. Guide students to recognize that they don't get all the information on each child at once. The book is organized by topic. New information about each child is presented as each topic is introduced.

3. After children have completed their charts, let them share information within their groups, and then with the class. They may notice that the charts are not all the same.

A Day in My Life (Language Arts, Social Studies)

Invite students to write and illustrate stories about a typical day in their lives. By following the organization of *Wake Up, World!* they can more easily compare and contrast their lives with those of children in the book.

1. Use copy paper to make a blank book for each child. Copy headings from the book on chart paper: "Our World," "Wake Up!" and so on.

2. Have students leave the first page blank (they can return to it later to create a cover). On the next page, have them copy the first heading, then draw a picture of themselves (or paste a photo) and write a caption that tells about their name. Have students continue on each page to tell the story of a typical day in their lives, paralleling the stories told by the children in the book.

Mapping Connections (Social Studies, Language Arts)

Semantic maps help readers make sense of information they read.

1. Explain that semantic maps are a form of note taking, and they do not need to display all the information in a book, just the broad, important concepts.

2. Together, create a semantic map for a country featured in the book (see sample, right). Point out that each "spoke" has a different set of details on it. But all of the information relates to the main topic (how children in that country live). To go further, children can work with partners to create new semantic maps based on the book.

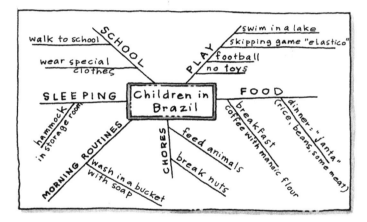

The author of *Wake Up, World!* does a wonderful job of telling the stories of the children around the world in language that most children can understand. A few vocabulary terms may be less familiar. Read the following words with students, model pronunciation, and have students say the words with you: *climate*, *customs*, and *traditions*.

Revisit pages in the book that use these words. Have students use text and illustrations as clues to tell what the words mean. Invite students to make the words their own by using them in the context of their lives. For example, have students describe the climate where they live. Repeat with customs and traditions.

Name _____

Date _____

Children Around the World Chart

Country: _____

Child: _____

Sleeping	Morning Routines	School	Play	Chores	Food

64